"*Down Mount Kenya on a Tea Tray* is a hugely enjoyable story that deals sensitively with the issue of obesity in children. It will appeal to a range of children, both girls and boys, as well as confident readers and those less so, who need coaxing to read. The setting of the story in Kenya provides a multi-cultural element that adds to its strengths, as well as a skilful and empathetic portrayal of the characters in the story. It would be an exciting addition to any school library, either as a stand-alone book or as a story to be used by teachers in a learning environment to raise awareness of the problems accompanying the condition of childhood obesity."

Emma Morton,
Educational Consultant, Nairobi

"A sensitive topic, dealt with honestly and compassionately. A story that starts with the main character reluctantly recognising a significant life challenge that he needs to face amidst his tragedy, how he sets a goal for himself and then, responding positively as those around him who join forces to support him, he experiences the life change that he needed. An inspiring story with adventure and humour, reflecting the journey and wonder of friendship, and that, with the will, and the support, mountains, both literal and figurative, can be climbed! This is a wonderful read."

Caro Strover,
Educational Psychologist

T0333413

Down Mount Kenya on a Tea Tray

Wesley had never thought much about his lifestyle or how he looked. He enjoyed eating his way through weekends in front of the telly with his mum. However, fate catapults him to a new life in East Africa and he is forced to face the negative impact that obesity is having on his life. When he rashly promises to climb Mount Kenya along with the rest of his class, an adventure in courage and determination begins . . .

This entertaining story explores some of the challenges faced by obese children and young people. It highlights both the physical limitations as well as the psychological problems associated with obesity, such as social isolation and low mood. The story explores the complicated web of factors that might cause a child to become obese and identifies some of the life-altering changes that can come from a healthy diet and active lifestyle.

Teaching lessons about kindness, friendship, bravery and determination, this is powerful reading for all children. It operates as a stand-alone story and is also available as part of a set along with a supporting guide.

Plum Hutton is a chartered educational psychologist and former learning support teacher. She holds a doctorate in educational psychology. She has more than 15 years of experience working as a local authority educational psychologist and latterly has transferred to independent practice. Through her work she has pursued and delivered training on many areas of professional interest, including supporting children with persistent anxiety, attachment difficulties, literacy difficulties and sensory processing differences.

Plum is a keen storyteller. She has gathered inspiration for her writing from her work, the challenges of parenthood and also through a nomadic existence as an Army wife, which has taken her to many locations across the UK and as far afield as East Africa.

Adventures with Diversity

**An Adventure with Autism and Social
Communication Difficulties:
The Man-Eating Sofa Storybook and Guidebook**
The Man-Eating Sofa: An Adventure with
Autism and Social Communication Difficulties
Supporting Autism and Social Communication
Difficulties in Mainstream Schools:
A Guidebook for *The Man-Eating Sofa*

**An Adventure with Dyslexia and Literacy Difficulties:
A Nasty Dose of the Yawns Storybook and Guidebook**
A Nasty Dose of the Yawns: An Adventure with
Dyslexia and Literacy Difficulties
Supporting Dyslexia and Literacy Difficulties in Schools:
A Guidebook for *A Nasty Dose of the Yawns*

**An Adventure with Childhood Obesity:
Down Mount Kenya on a Tea Tray Storybook and Guidebook**
Down Mount Kenya on a Tea Tray: An Adventure with
Childhood Obesity
Supporting Childhood Obesity in Schools:
A Guidebook for *Down Mount Kenya on a Tea Tray*

Down Mount Kenya on a Tea Tray

An Adventure with Childhood Obesity

Plum Hutton

Illustrated by Freddie Hodge

Routledge
Taylor & Francis Group

LONDON AND NEW YORK

Cover image: Freddie Hodge

First published 2022
by Routledge
2 Park Square, Milton Park, Abingdon, Oxon OX14 4RN

and by Routledge
605 Third Avenue, New York, NY 10158

Routledge is an imprint of the Taylor & Francis Group, an informa business

British Library Cataloguing-in-Publication Data
A catalogue record for this book is available from the British Library

Library of Congress Cataloging-in-Publication Data
A catalog record has been requested for this book

ISBN: 978-1-032-07622-5 (pbk)
ISBN: 978-1-003-20798-6 (ebk)

DOI: 10.4324/9781003207986

Typeset in Helvetica and Avenir
by Deanta Global Publishing Services, Chennai, India

To Iona and Ramsay – for their grit and determination while climbing Mount Kenya and for being crazy enough to swim in Lake Michaelson before breakfast.

Contents

Acknowledgements   xi
Author's note   xii

Prologue   1

Chapter One   5

Chapter Two   14

Chapter Three   25

Chapter Four   45

Chapter Five   52

Chapter Six   60

Chapter Seven   69

Chapter Eight   84

Chapter Nine   90

Chapter Ten   100

Chapter Eleven   110

Chapter Twelve   125

Chapter Thirteen   134

Chapter Fourteen   139

Epilogue   142

Acknowledgements

I would like to extend my thanks to:

Iona and Ramsay Hutton for their encouragement and youthful perspective

Dr Kate Rennie, Claire Anson, Karin Twiss, Emma Judge and Fran Townend for their support and advice

Alex Hutton for his patience, optimism and support during the writing of this book.

Author's note

This story includes some frank descriptions of an obese child. It felt uncomfortable writing so bluntly about a child being overweight. The portrayal is not intended to make fun of obese children or to judge them. Instead, the aim is to raise awareness of the scale of the issue and the serious psychological and physical impact that obesity can have on children's lives. The World Health Organization estimated in 2019 that, worldwide, over 38 million children (under the age of five) were overweight or obese. In the UK in 2017, it was estimated that a third of children aged between two and fifteen years old were overweight or obese, which has long-term consequences for their personal health. Therefore, it is argued that it is important to be able to discuss childhood obesity openly and to provide support for children who would like to make positive changes in their lives.

This is a work of fiction. Unless otherwise indicated, all the names, characters, events and incidents in this book are either the product of the author's imagination or used in a fictitious manner. Any resemblance to actual persons, living or dead, or actual events is purely coincidental.

Prologue

The plane lurched as it bumped through the clouds, gradually descending towards Nairobi airport. Wesley clutched the arms of his seat, utterly terrified. He was not particularly concerned if the plane crashed. That would just put an end to everything, which would make his situation much easier. But the sinking aircraft signified that the end of his journey was near, and he was not ready for his future life, which was hurtling towards him like an avalanche. Captain Halliday yawned and let his head slump again to the other side.

Wesley closed his eyes, struggling to absorb all the changes in his life. He could still see the image of Mrs Hawthorn's smiling face, starting that unforgettable conversation back in Yorkshire.

"It's wonderful news, Wesley. You're going to live with your father," Mrs Hawthorn had said. Wesley stared at his new foster carer in disbelief.

"But I haven't got a father," he pointed out. The social worker with the kind eyes had smiled her patient smile and slowly explained.

"Wesley, we've found out that your mother was still married when you were born, although your parents separated just before your mother realised she was pregnant with you. Your father is called Peter MacKay. He's a sergeant in the Army." Wesley had not known what to say to this news, so he said nothing. The social worker had continued in her annoyingly calm voice.

"Wesley, your dad is your next of kin and he's agreed to look after you." She paused, waiting for a response, but Wesley was too numb for any of this information to penetrate his brain. "It's very exciting, Wesley. He is currently working in Kenya, training soldiers for the British Army. So you'll be moving to Africa." The tone of her voice made it sound like a lovely afternoon treat, rather than being exiled from his familiar life, in order to live with a man he had never met.

The plane bumped again through another layer of clouds. This time, the movement jerked Captain Halliday's head so much that he snapped awake. He glanced out of the window at the outskirts of Nairobi, visible in the early-morning light, and then smiled at Wesley.

"Not long now," he said encouragingly. Wesley scowled at him for assuming that the end of the journey would be a good thing. He looked down at his body squashed uncomfortably into the airline seat and again felt a surge of dread. What would his father think of him? In the past, he had never worried about his appearance. He had accepted his body for what it was. But that had all changed when he heard that he was going to meet his father, and that his father was in the Army. His father would be fit. He would be tough. He would expect his son to be the same. Wesley had stood in front of the mirror in his bedroom at Mrs Hawthorn's house and inspected his reflection with new eyes. He noticed the way in which his chin seemed to flow into his neck; how he drooped around his waist and thighs. He stared furiously at his reflection confirming the thought that buzzed round his brain like a persistent wasp. *Peter MacKay is not going to love me. Peter MacKay won't even like me.*

Pete shifted restlessly from one foot to another, feeling conspicuous in his army uniform. He was not good at keeping still, even when he was calm, and he was currently as jumpy as a cricket. The airport screens clearly said that the flight from Heathrow had landed ten minutes ago. He scanned the crowd of people flowing into the arrivals hall, looking for Bill Halliday's familiar face. He turned and paced away a short distance, desperately trying to control his nerves. As so often happened with him, fear turned to frustration, and he cursed Fate for having landed him in such a ridiculous situation. Ten days ago, he had not known he had a son, and here he was, standing in an East African airport about to meet him. Normal people didn't start parenthood in an airport, Pete thought bitterly, clenching his jaw. He couldn't believe that this had happened while his passport was being renewed, so he hadn't even been able to travel back to the UK to meet Wesley. He felt totally unqualified to be a father. Fighting in Afghanistan had been less frightening than this. Then, he had felt scared but in control, trained to do the right thing. Now, he felt bewildered. He had no idea what made eleven-year-old boys tick.

He took a deep breath and turned back to the rail, which kept the relatives at bay, as a new wave of arrivals emerged from the baggage reclaim area. He saw a hand raised in greeting and recognised Bill Halliday pushing a trolley through the crowds. Pete strained to see the smaller figure walking beside Bill, but a family was blocking his view. He moved through the crowd so that he could see his son for the first time. Their eyes met briefly, and Pete encountered Wesley's look of loathing, before the boy turned away. Pete studied his son's form, desperately trying to control the panic rising inside him. One look at Wesley had told him that this was going to be even harder than he had anticipated. Pete closed his eyes momentarily, praying to any deity that might be listening for the strength to cope. He breathed deeply, bravely mustered a smile and moved forward to greet his son for the first time.

Chapter One

When Wesley ambled across the playground of his new school, he knew it would be a disaster. This was not because it was four thousand miles away from his previous school or because he could not pronounce any of the teachers' names. Rather, he knew it would be awful because school, for him, was usually awful. He understood now what people thought of him. He had seen the flash of revulsion on his father's face at the airport. It had only been there for a second, before Pete composed his expression into kindly smiles, but that first impression had been unmistakable.

Wesley glanced across the grass courtyard surrounded on three sides by classrooms. The grass was green and lush. Great banks of vibrantly coloured flowers covered lines of bushes that formed a border between the playground and paved areas outside each classroom. A large group of children, of a variety of ages, was playing tag. He noted how the older ones charitably allowed a tiny scrap of a girl to catch them, much to her delight. Other children were chatting and laughing, punctuating their stories with great sweeping hand movements and shaking giggles. It seemed to be a happy place, he thought miserably.

The children were unusually varied compared with his old school. The most common words were in English, but he picked out other languages being articulated on the playground – perhaps French, Kiswahili and a couple more that he did not recognise. He liked the fact that the children all looked different. Some were small with rich, shiny skin like conkers; others had darker skin. Some had no hair, whereas lots had long multi-coloured braids, and several little blond children scampered about with their tanned skin glowing like hot toast in the sun. An Asian boy ran past, towing his sister behind him. Her long black hair rippled like a silken scarf down beyond her waist.

Yet despite this unusual picture of diversity, he could sense he was alone, the odd one out, a magnet for curious, staring eyes. Wesley was clearly the only child in this school who was obese.

"Great," he muttered to himself. "This is going to be even worse than the last place."

The bell rang and the playground emptied, as the children disappeared to their classes. Miss Omwoto, the headteacher, gestured for him to follow her across the playground to the Year 6 class, and he shuffled after her. He felt the sweat trickling down between his thighs with each step. She spoke in a soft voice but with such a strong accent that he found it hard to understand the usual barrage of questions: *How was his journey? Where was he living? Where had he been to school?* And so on. He was aware that she did not seem to know quite where to look, and he imagined what she might be thinking, rather than focusing on what she was actually saying. He could almost sense her thoughts travelling from her brain to his. *So, you're Wesley. I had no idea you would be so huge! How did you get sooo fat? I mean, you really are enormous. I could probably fit my whole family at once in your underwear! Can you run? Oh, gracious! PE is going to be difficult. I doubt any of the other children will like him. Good grief, he has six chins when he smiles. How have his parents let him get so fat?*

He was relieved when they reached the classroom and Miss Omwoto introduced him to a tall, thin woman with a crooked smile, called Mrs Wambui. She looked a little taken aback when she saw him but managed to welcome him appropriately.

"Welcome to Year Six, Wesley," Mrs Wambui said. "Your desk is next to Isla, so she will show you around today until you find your feet." *She's probably wondering when I last saw my feet*, Wesley sighed to himself. He looked across at the empty desk and could immediately see the first problem. The desks were old-fashioned with a lid that opened to reveal the schoolbooks and a chair attached. The gap between the chair and the desk was plentiful for an average child, but Wesley doubted that his very un-average bottom was going to fit. There was some hurried whispering between the two teachers, and Miss Omwoto rushed off to find the caretaker. Mrs Wambui seemed paralysed, as Wesley stood next to his appointed desk unable to squeeze his bulk on to the chair. He tried to ignore the staring eyes of the other nine children, who were already seated. Suddenly, a voice from beside him ventured,

"Mrs Wambui, I wonder if Wesley might be more comfortable if he sat at the craft table on your chair? I'm not sure that the class chairs are quite the right size for him?"

Wesley looked to his right where a tall, slim girl was smiling at him. She had wide blue eyes and a pale, heart-shaped face with freckles sprinkled across her nose. She was already moving Miss Wambui's chair over to the craft table on the far side of her desk.

"These desks aren't very flexible," she said apologetically. "My legs are too long for them. I think you might find it a bit of a squash."

Wesley looked across at his new classmate. He felt a warm glow flooding down to his fingertips. She had been kind! She had acknowledged his problem without humiliating him, and that was something he would remember for ever. He smiled back.

"I'm Isla. Welcome to Nanyuki," she continued. "There are only ten of us in Year Six, so I'm sure you'll soon get to know everyone."

From there, the day had improved. The children in his class were generally pleasant. There were six girls and only three other boys. Christopher seemed pretty bonkers. He had a mass of black curly hair that appeared to have a life of its own. It swayed and danced as he became excited about almost every word Mrs Wambui said. The other two boys were more of a worry. They were fit and lean and obviously made a powerful team. Simon was very blond with nut-brown skin and deep green eyes. He moved with quick, fluid motions, obviously comfortable in his skin. Wesley noticed that Simon wrote and drew swiftly and confidently. Also, he was quick to complete all the sums in maths. He had a sinking feeling that Simon was going to be amazing at everything, which made Wesley feel even more inadequate than usual. Neil was clearly Simon's best friend. Wesley could not fail to notice the meaningful glances that the two boys exchanged throughout the morning, puffing out their cheeks and laughing when they thought no one was looking. His fears were fulfilled at break time. The bell went and Simon was the first out of the classroom. He took a huge leap over the bushes in front of the class and flicked over twice on landing, like a professional gymnast. He was followed by Neil and a herd of Year 5 boys, who grabbed a football and headed out on to the field.

The girls showed Wesley where to get a snack and then began practising their songs for the school concert the following week. Wesley wandered off and sat in the shade of an ancient bus, which doubled as a climbing frame. He sat, wallowing in self-pity, ignoring the swarm of Early Years children who seemed to think that the bus was a sinking ship. Despite Isla's kindness, he knew that this school would be terrible. School always was. He was huge and ugly and uninteresting. No one would want to be his friend. After all, his mother hadn't wanted to be his mother, he thought savagely, so why would anyone else want to love him?

"Isn't she beautiful?" said a small voice. "I'm dead, so I can't play anymore."

"Huh?" replied Wesley, somewhat confused.

"Yes. I fell off the boat and got eaten by a shark, so I can't play again until the others get killed. It's the rules," explained his new companion, who sat down beside him with her short legs sticking straight out in front. "She's always beautiful in the mornings," continued the little girl. Wesley felt muddled; he'd only just realised what she'd meant about being eaten by a shark. She sat very still, staring into the distance, so he followed her gaze across the playing field, where a few goats and a cow grazed lazily in the morning sun, on across the houses at the edge of town, until he suddenly saw her. Emerging out of the jungle, with a wreath of cloud swathed across her shoulders, the craggy summit of Mount Kenya rose majestically into the crisp blue sky.

"She's often shy in the afternoon and hides behind the clouds, so I like to watch her in the morning," his new friend explained. They sat in companionable silence, staring at the mountain above.

"Yay! They're all dead – that means I can play again," she squealed. Suddenly, the tiny girl jumped to her feet. She scrambled up the side of the bus with a horde of little friends, ready to invent the next catastrophe. Wesley sat staring at the two peaks in the distance. The snow glinted where it clung to the sheer rocks. He had never imagined seeing snow on the equator. The summit looked bleak, dangerous and menacing, but he had to agree. She was beautiful.

"Yes, Sir. That's right. It all happened rather suddenly." Pete looked across at his boss. Major Foster was about the same age as Sergeant Pete MacKay, but their experiences of life were probably very different, Pete thought to himself wryly. Henry Foster was well spoken, well educated, had an attractive and intelligent wife and two perfect children. *Not scum of the earth like me*, thought Pete. He'd never known his parents and spent most of his childhood in a variety of foster homes. He'd joined the Army at the age of sixteen, really because he'd not known what else to do. To his surprise, he found that the Army had been not just a successful career but a family for him as well. He had found friends and security through his work, and the rigid rules and structures were a relief after his chaotic start in life.

"Would it help to talk about it?" Major Foster asked. Pete paused.

"Well, if you've got the time, Sir, I think it would." He drew a deep breath, deciding that it would be best to lurch through the story as quickly as possible. "I met the boy's mother about fourteen years ago when I was in Catterick, Yorkshire. We married too quickly, I suppose, but it seemed a good idea at the time. Looking back, we didn't have much in common and it all ended when I got posted to Germany. She said she didn't want to move, and we went our separate ways. I didn't know she'd had a son; she never told me." He looked up, wondering if he would see disapproval in his boss's face, but all he observed was genuine concern. So Pete blundered on. "I got a call about three weeks ago to say that her body had been found, and I was named as the boy's father." He trailed off for a moment, remembering the electrifying blow of the phone call, which in a few short minutes had turned his life upside down, made him a father and left his ex-wife dead.

"What a terrible shock. Parenthood still takes me by surprise and I've had eleven years of practice," the major remarked, lightening the mood a little.

Pete smiled gratefully. "I have to admit, Sir, it's a steep learning curve. I've never had to deal with a child before. The Colonel's found a house for us, but I'm used to eating with the guys. Now I have to cook for us both, and sort out school uniform, and be home to meet the school bus. I've no idea who'll look after him in the holidays."

"Well, we've got a while to think about that. He's in the same class as Isla, so I'm sure Anna will take him out on some trips with our two," Major Foster replied. "How has he coped with moving out to Kenya? It would have been easier for him if you had been working in the UK when all this happened?" Pete paused, twisting his beret in his hands.

"Hmm. He's not coping too well. I don't think either of us are, if I'm honest, Sir. The thing is . . ." He hesitated, unsure of how to go on. "I'm not sure how to deal with this really, but Wesley is clinically obese. I mean he's not just solid like me. He is so overweight he can hardly walk. I'm not sure he'd be able to go walking and swimming and all the things that your kids do in the holidays."

"Kids! What a terrible Americanism; you make it sound as though I have spawned baby goats. I have children not kids, Sergeant Mac. You should know that by now!" snorted the major.

"How could I forget?" laughed the sergeant, rolling his eyes in despair. Precise use of language was one of Major Foster's more annoying quirks. Henry Foster became serious for a moment.

"I'm sure that Welfare Support and the Medical Centre will be able to provide some help. But if there is anything I can do, please let me know. I'm not just saying that to be polite," he continued, "I really mean it." Pete looked across at the man with whom he'd spent many nights out in the bush, eating rations in the dust, shaving out of mess tins at first light each morning. The man who took everything in his stride, who understood difficult situations and yet did not dwell on them. Pete suddenly had a feeling that everything might be all right, after all.

"Thank you, Sir. But I warn you, I might need all the help I can get."

Chapter Two

Wesley was at school early the following morning, having arrived on the school bus. He flopped on the bench in the playground, watching other children arrive. A gentle whirring filled the air, like a purposeful insect, and he saw a dark smudge approach across the morning sky from the north. He assumed that it was one of the military helicopters that were used for taking casualties down to the hospital in Nairobi. But the small aircraft headed straight for the school and swiftly descended to land neatly on the sports pitch.

A lithe figure jumped out, school bag slung across his shoulder. He walked briskly away from the turning blades and did not look back, as the chopper lifted off again, banking round to head north towards the Lolldaiga Hills. To his disgust, Wesley saw that it was Simon approaching and that he was soon surrounded by a knot of chattering children. Wesley seethed with the unfairness of it all. Not only was Simon clever, sporty, popular and thin, but to top

     DOI: 10.4324/9781003207986-3

it all he came to school by helicopter, which meant he was rich and cool. Life just wasn't fair!

Sergeant Mary Sunningdale chewed her lip as she surveyed the weighing machine. She made a note of the weight and looked across at the boy, who had slowly shuffled over to sit on the chair in the corner of the clinic room. Looking down at the figures again, she wondered if the elderly chair would cope with his weight. In all her years as a military nurse, she had never had to deal with such an obese child, and the situation frustrated her. This child did not have an injury or a tropical disease or some developmental disorder. However, it looked as though he might eat himself to death if he did not rapidly lose some weight. She suddenly felt tired and pinched the bridge of her nose to relieve the nagging headache that had been building up all afternoon. It was nearly five p.m. and there was still a queue of people in the waiting room.

Mary had been up most of the night caring for a little girl with a high fever. The doctor suspected meningitis and knew that they did not have the facilities to treat her in Nanyuki, but patients could not be evacuated until first light. Mary had spent the early hours of the morning monitoring the limp body with its racing heart and fine hair hanging in sweat-soaked tendrils down her neck. Mary had held the weeping mother in her arms when the gravity of the situation had overwhelmed her. Mary had stood in the half-light of dawn watching the pale faces of the doctor and mother staring down through the side window of the helicopter, as it turned steeply away from the sports pitch on its journey south. With one of the doctors away in Nairobi, it was even busier than usual, and Mary only just had time for breakfast and a change of clothes before the day began.

Now, here was Wesley MacKay, slouched sullenly in the corner of her clinic room. His father, Pete, was shifting uncomfortably from foot to foot and seemed reluctant to look at his son or meet her eye. She drew a deep breath.

"Well, Wesley, I'm afraid you are clinically obese." She paused, waiting for the meaning of her words to sink in.

Wesley looked up at her and defiantly shot back, "Yeah, as if I hadn't noticed. Tell me something I don't know!" Mary clenched her fists, trying not to lose her temper, and then decided to give it to him straight.

"OK, you asked for it," she replied. "You are dangerously overweight. You are eating too much of the wrong type of food and not taking enough exercise," she added ruefully. "You are at increased risk of disability and dying young. You are at increased risk of cancer, having heart disease, as well as breathing difficulties both during the day and when you sleep. You are at risk of developing type two diabetes, which can lead to serious and unpleasant complications. As you reach adolescence, you are more likely to have low self-esteem and a poor quality of life. You are likely to develop joint problems such as foot, ankle and knee pain, and so have problems with everyday activities such as walking and climbing stairs. It is estimated that treating obesity cost the NHS about six billion pounds last year, which is pretty outrageous considering it could be largely prevented if people adopted a healthier lifestyle."

Mary could feel that she had gone red in the face and some saliva had sprayed on to her desk as she had spat out the last sentence. Wesley and Pete were staring directly at her now through an eerie silence that slowly circled the room. She looked down at her desk, suddenly ashamed of her outburst. She knew that this boy's life had been difficult and that his lifestyle would have been determined by the adults in his life, rather than his choice.

"I'm sorry," she said, aghast at her own behaviour. "That was totally unprofessional. I should never have been so blunt." To her surprise, Pete responded immediately.

"Actually, I think it was what we both needed to hear. The question is, what are we going to do about it?"

Father and son drove out of the army camp in silence, both trying to recover from the shock of Mary's outburst and the harsh advice she had given them. It was hard to know what to say when they faced a challenge that they needed to solve together, and yet had no bond or common ground on which to form a plan. They had no real understanding of each other's feelings or motivations. Worse still, they did not even like each other.

Wesley sat staring straight ahead, not seeing the motorbikes – or boda bodas, as they seemed to be called – streaming around the car. *I am not going on a diet*, he fumed to himself. In the last few weeks, his life had been turned upside down. His mum had abandoned him, and he'd been dragged away from his home and school to live in this smelly, dusty, pathetic excuse for a town. The internet hardly ever worked. Even his Xbox wasn't reliable because the electricity often went off. He liked eating, he enjoyed eating, he thought about eating most hours of the day. He was not going to let some wizened old nurse take away the one thing he really enjoyed and was really good at. Eating made him feel better. It was his only comfort, and he wasn't going to start tucking into healthy brown rice and lentils. *My life is rubbish*, he thought bitterly, *and nothing will make it better.*

Pete also stared at the road, but he was very aware of the numerous hazards it presented as he manoeuvred the vehicle through the oncoming traffic. There were boda bodas everywhere tonight, as people headed home before dark. One sped past with four farmworkers wedged on the back; the next carried a whole family, with the father steering round a toddler in his lap and a small child grasping at his waist. His wife perched side saddle with a baby strapped to her back, blinking dazedly through the dust. Pete swerved to avoid the sofa approaching rapidly down the high street. The man sitting on the sofa seemed totally calm, even when the boda boda supporting it hit a pothole, and the whole contraption began to capsize to the left. The driver fought to control the bike but could not resist gravity. The sofa, motorbike and both men slowly keeled over into the roadside drainage ditch. Pete drove swiftly past, knowing it was best not to get involved, and anyway he had enough problems of his own at the moment.

He felt completely lost. Three weeks ago, he unexpectedly became the father of an eleven-year-old boy. A boy he had no idea existed. He had never wanted to have children; his job was busy enough without added complications. He liked having a room in the Sergeants' Mess and eating with his friends in the evening. He was good at his job, confident and authoritative, but he had no idea how to be a parent to this boy. He glanced across at Wesley, who was slouched against the door of the car. *How on earth could they be related?* They seemed to have nothing in common at all. Pete had had to move out of the Mess and into a house because of this boy. The Army had provided basic furniture, but Pete had never had to cook for himself before and had certainly never had to cook for someone on a diet. He had liked his life the way it was, and if he was really frank, he was embarrassed to be seen with Wesley. Pete had worked hard all his adult life. How could he respect an ungrateful lump of a boy, who wanted to do nothing but eat and watch TV? Moodily, he swung the car into the Nakumatt carpark and was waved into a space by the uniformed guard.

"Come on, Wesley," muttered Pete gruffly. "This is the main supermarket in town. We'd better get some food."

It was the first time Wesley had been into a Kenyan supermarket. In many ways, it was just like Asda or Tesco in the UK, but as they pushed the trolley up the aisles, he began to notice the differences. Some of the shelves were empty, others stocked with products that he had never seen before, such as strange types of cooking oil, maize flour and dog rice. There were rows and rows of black hair extensions, and haircare products featuring beautiful African women with shiny hair and radiant skin. Several men were beating the goods with large feather dusters as if the cans and packets needed to be punished.

Pete put on a positive smile.

"So, what do you like for breakfast?" he asked.

"Cereal," replied Wesley sullenly.

"Right, well, that should be fairly simple," said Pete, peering down the aisles, looking for the cereal section. When they found it, Pete could see that cereal was not going to be a simple option. Wesley was desperately scanning the shelves for Coco Pops, which were obviously unobtainable. He looked despondently down the line of porridge and Sunnybisk, which seemed to be an approximation of Weetabix. He finally spotted a UK brand he recognised – Crunchy Nut Cornflakes. He grabbed the box and dumped it in the trolley. Pete winced, wondering how much sugar the cereal contained. He looked at the price and swallowed hard. It was nearly £10 a packet, and a packet was not going to last long, judging by Wesley's waistline. He would have to talk to Wesley about the expense of imported food. Wesley had moved on and was loading three large bottles of fizzy drinks into the trolley. Pete was quick to challenge him.

"I don't think that fizzy pop is a good idea if you are on a diet," he said, swiftly returning the bottles to the shelves. "Let's find some milk for the cereal and get some fruit. The papaws are good out here." Wesley scowled at his father's back and then looked longingly at a giant bottle of Coke. He had only had water to drink all day and could murder a good slug of Coke. Quickly, he turned his back on his father and grabbed the Coke off the shelf. The lid was stiff but soon came free with a firm twist. Wesley tipped up the bottle and started glugging the contents. It was so fizzy that it was hard to drink fast, and the bubbles began to go up his nose, but he revelled in the sweetness of the liquid and felt a flood of power course through his veins. His father could say what he liked, but he couldn't ban him from drinking what he wanted, when he wanted. Defiantly, he screwed the lid back on, sauntered over to Pete and dropped the half-empty bottle into the trolley. Pete stared at the bottle and suddenly flushed red.

"Why, you little tyke!" he thundered. "How dare you?" He felt an urge to thump the boy on his podgy nose, which was how he had tended to solve arguments when he was younger. Instead, he stood breathing deeply and gripping the trolley so fiercely that his knuckles went white. The two faced each other across the trolley, eyes blazing. Finally, still shaking with anger, Pete turned away towards the vegetable section.

By the time they reached the checkout, both the soldier and the boy were close to breaking point. Pete stared despondently at the relatively healthy food he had in the trolley, which he did not know how to cook. Wesley stared at the disgusting contents of the trolley, which included no chips, pizza or anything that he considered to be edible, apart from the half-drunk bottle of Coke, which taunted him from the corner. Then Wesley's eye was caught by an array of chocolate bars next to the checkout. They were all British brands that he recognised and loved. He could almost hear them calling to him in low seductive voices:

Come on, eat me! No, eat me! I'm even tastier. I've got peanuts. Yes, but you get two bars for the price of one if you choose me. Try my tasty caramel. Go on! You know you want to!

His mouth watered. He could not choose between them – they all looked delicious. With a sweep of his hand, he thrust twenty or so bars into the trolley, already fantasising about how they would taste if he ate them all on the way home in the car.

Pete was furious. "Oh no, you don't! You're not pulling another fast one on me," he barked. "Look at you! How are you going to lose weight if you eat that lot?" He gesticulated wildly at the smattering of chocolate that littered the top of the trolley.

"I don't want to lose weight!" Wesley flashed back. "I'm just fine the way I am. And who are you to order me around? You're not my dad. Dads don't abandon their families for twelve years. Where were you when Mum found things difficult? Where were you when she was ill? You can bog off and stick your healthy food right up your arse!" he yelled, before turning tail and waddling out of the shop. Pete was completely stunned. His authority had not been challenged for years. In the Army, if you told someone to do something, they just did it.

"Oi! Come back here!" he bellowed at the back of his departing son, but the boy disappeared around the corner.

Pete then began to panic. The food was half checked through the till, so he couldn't leave without paying. He wanted to follow Wesley to make sure he was all right, but he was worried about completely losing his temper if the boy wound him up any further. He was aware of all the other shoppers staring at him, making judgements. His thoughts were running wild. *I can't do this. I don't like this boy. I don't want this boy. I can't afford this boy.* His thoughts tumbled over each other. *I am responsible for him, and he knows nothing about Kenya. It's not safe for him to be alone out on the street. I have to find him. I have to find him!*

"Pete?" He felt a hand on his shoulder as he frantically stuffed food into shopping bags. He spun round to be faced with Anna, Major Foster's wife. He could not identify his emotions when he saw her. They included a flood of relief, followed by anger and then anxiety. Had Anna seen what had just happened? Had she seen big, tough Pete MacKay humiliated by an eleven-year-old boy? Anna spoke again.

"Pete, it's OK. He hasn't gone far. He's just outside. I've left Isla and Freddie with him."

Pete paused with a papaw halfway to the shopping bag.

"Anna, I can't do this. I don't know how to be a father." Anna fixed him with a steady gaze.

"Look," she said calmly. "This situation would challenge any adult. It is a nightmare for you both, but you are doing fine. You can do it, and you will do it." She gave Pete a playful punch on the arm. "You know what Henry would say?" Pete shook his head numbly. "Toughen up, buttercup!"

He smiled wryly. Of course that is what Major Foster would say. 'Motivating' phrases were another of his annoying habits.

Anna continued, "Now, get your shopping sorted. I've got a plan."

Wesley stood miserably outside Nakumatt, aware of the tears streaking down his chin. He could feel Isla's hand on his shoulder. She wasn't saying anything, but he was glad she was there. He was ashamed of what he had said. He was ashamed of crying in front of all the passers-by, but he felt utterly wretched.

Then, through the fog of his misery, he realised that someone was calling his name. He looked up to see a tall woman in a peacock-coloured skirt. She held out her hand and it was a moment before he realised that he should shake it in greeting.

"Hello, Wesley. My name is Anna. I am Isla's mum." Wesley sniffed and made to wipe his nose on his sleeve but realised he was wearing a short-sleeved top. Anna delved into her bag and retrieved a tissue, which she handed to him.

"Your dad and Isla's dad are both working tomorrow, so I am going to take you all out to the river for a picnic." Wesley did not know what to say to this. She had not asked him if he would like to come but just told him that he was coming. Obviously, she was another adult to boss him around. A picnic at the river – she had to be joking. A river was the last place in the world that he would like to visit. He would prefer to just be left alone with his Xbox, but that did not seem to be an option.

Anna went on talking, "I'll pick you up at nine in the morning. You'll need a change of clothes and your swimming trunks. I assume you can swim?" Wesley nodded mutely. "Great," she said brightly. "Right now, I think your dad needs a hand with the shopping." She gestured towards Pete who was leaving the shop, laden with carrier bags.

Wesley sniffed and blew his nose loudly. Anna looked him solemnly in the eye, before suddenly smiling and throwing him a casual wink. "We'll see you in the morning," she said over her shoulder as she headed for her car.

I'm not going, thought Wesley mutinously. *She can't make me.* But there was something about the way she had winked at him that made him realise he would go, even though he knew he wouldn't enjoy it.

Chapter Three

Saturday dawned the same as most days in Nanyuki, cool, clear and everything sparkling as the sun crept up and over the flanks of Mount Kenya. Anna clutched her tea, warming her fingers on the mug. She loved to lurk on the balcony for just a few minutes each morning, watching the mountain silhouetted in the rising sun. There was something about the mountain that was comforting, the knowledge that she was always there, even when the clouds drifted down her sides so that she looked like an ancient smoking volcano. Anna idly studied the mousebirds perched on the branches of the trees behind the garden. They looked like micro-pheasants, no larger than a robin, but with splendid long tails, which hung below the branches. She loved Nanyuki's early-morning sounds. The ruckus of the pigs being fed and the cows impatient to be let loose on the roadside verges to graze. The neighbour's cockerel, which seemed to crow at all hours of day and night. Then the deafening caw of the ibises, who stalked around on long, rugged legs, dipping their huge, curved beaks into the grass in search of bugs. They would be ugly birds were it not for their shimmering green wings, which they would stretch before swooping noisily into the trees. In the house behind her, a clock chimed, interrupting her reverie. *Hmm*, she thought. *This won't do. I'd better get a move on if we're picking Wesley up at nine.*

An hour later, they were on the road. Isla, her brother Freddie and his friend Thomas in the back seat. Wesley sat in the front, mainly because Anna wasn't sure he would fit in the back comfortably. They took the road running north

DOI: 10.4324/9781003207986-4 **25**

out of Nanyuki, past the little village of Jua Kali until the tarmac road abruptly ended and they began to rattle along the stone track through the bush.

Wesley had decided that he was not going to enjoy the day. He did not want to play happy families with people he hardly knew. He was totally unaccustomed to the rough Kenyan roads and could feel his belly undulating over each bump and pothole. The other three children chatted incessantly about people they knew and places they had been. He did not feel that he had anything interesting to add to the conversation, so he sat staring glumly at the track ahead.

As they rounded a corner, Anna suddenly slowed and pointed to the left of the car.

"Look!" she said.

Wesley stared into the bush, just seeing dry earth and scrubby trees. The ground was covered in places with lush grass and some delicate blue flowers, which he assumed had sprung up since the recent rains. It was pretty, but the scene did not seem to warrant stopping the car. Then a movement caught his eye. High up, above a small acacia tree, a face was watching him. Huge oval eyes gazed out between extravagant curling eyelashes. The long ears twitched occasionally to throw off passing insects. Two stubby horns were visible on top of the long face. But the most fascinating feature was a neat nose and hairy, nimble lips. As he watched, the giraffe relaxed and carefully drew back her lips to nibble the ends of a fearsomely prickly branch.

Anna gently indicated to the right of the car, and Wesley looked across the road to see five more tall necks rising from the bush. All were examining the car with interest rather than alarm. Looking back to the left, six more appeared, moving sedately through the bush, their long necks rocking forward as they walked. An enormous male seemed to be leading the herd across the road to join the others on the right. He slowly lolloped out on to the track, huge legs appearing to be moving in slow motion, but covering the ground swiftly with each giant step. Behind came the female that Wesley had first seen. She had a skittish baby at her side, who scuttled forward a few paces before stopping to stare and then rushing on again. Something spooked the remaining animals, and they broke into a lumbering canter, crossing the road like a gently rolling wave before turning to stare at the car one more time.

Isla leant forward and whispered, "They're reticulated giraffe. Pretty cool, aren't they?" Wesley was unable to answer. He had never seen anything so awe-inspiring in his life. Anna smiled to herself and started the car's engine.

A few miles further on, Freddie sighed, and they had to slow to a halt again.

"Not another zebra crossing! I'm dying for a swim." They waited as the large herd of common zebras raced across the road in front of them. Anna grinned.

"I never understand zebras. They will be grazing quite happily, but when they see a car coming, they feel the sudden desire to race across the road, right in front of the vehicle."

"Well, when you are that beautiful, I think you are allowed to be a bit nuts," commented Isla.

They wound on down the track through herds of impala, scattering tiny antelopes called dik-diks in their path. They stopped briefly to rescue a tortoise, which was a bit stuck in the ruts of the road. Isla leapt out and brought it round to show Wesley. The tortoise hissed menacingly through the car window and then weed down Isla's leg. Freddie and Thomas howled with laughter. Isla simply gave the tortoise a fierce look.

"That is no way to treat someone who is helping you," she said frostily, before placing him on the ground out of the way of the road.

They paused on the bridge over the river to look for hippos, but none were lounging in the pool that day. So Anna swung the car to the right, along a track that followed the river downstream, until she came to an area where the river widened out into a lazy flow, with sandy beaches on each side. Upstream was a small rapid, where the water plunged through a rocky gorge. Anna parked the car in the shade of an acacia tree and the three children in the back tumbled out.

Anna was serious for a moment. "Right, guys, you know the rules. One – have fun and that means that you need to stay safe, because if someone drowns, it is not fun anymore. Two – you stay in my sight. Three – if I give you an instruction, you follow it immediately."

"Yeah, yeah, we get it," squeaked Freddie and Thomas. "Can we swim? Can we swim?"

"Of course," laughed Anna. "Off you go."

Wesley skulked by the car for about half an hour after they arrived. He could hardly look at the river. His mind filled with terrible, desperate images every time he glanced at the oozing brown water. He could see fear, panic and pain swirling along the riverbed. So he stayed slumped against the car, only occasionally glancing at the others. Anna was busy sorting out the picnic and changing into her swimming costume. The other children had all plunged into the water, whooping and splashing each other. They spent some time swimming against the current and discovering hidden rocks beneath the surface. Now they were on the far bank, damming a side channel of river water. Isla called for Wesley to join them, but he hung back, not sure what to do.

Part of Wesley wanted to join in the fun, but he had only ever swum in a swimming pool before and the brown, eddying river water frightened him. It reminded him of the peaty waters of the River Swale in Yorkshire; of his last, bleak days in his mother's flat. It reminded him of memories and emotions that he could not dare to relive or put into words. Except that this river was different. Africa was different, almost like a new beginning.

It was impossible to see what was beneath the surface of the water, and he had visions of crocodiles and snakes lurking in the depths, waiting to pounce. He was also worried that he might not be able to swim well enough against the current to reach the other side. He could feel the sweat dripping between his shoulder blades, under his arms and between his thighs. The water did look cool and refreshing. However, despite his fears, his most insurmountable problem was that swimming would involve stripping down to his swimming trunks. He glanced across at Isla on the far bank, where she was cantering around like a foal, long legs leading to a streamlined body. Her brown hair spilt behind as she outran the smaller boys, who were chasing her with great handfuls of mud. She looked like a nymph playing in the shallows, and there was no way he was getting his kit off in front of her or anyone else.

"The brown water is a bit off-putting at first," stated Anna who had come to stand behind him. "The rivers round here are always brown due to the red earth that is swept down by the rain. But there are no hippos here; it is too shallow for them. No crocs either. You can see crocs in the river at Samburu, but we are much higher up here and they can't cope with the cold at night." They stood for a while watching the others play.

"Have you got a change of clothes with you?" asked Anna. Wesley nodded despondently. "Then I should swim in what you are wearing. It's good to keep a bit covered up so you don't get sunburnt. The sun is vicious out here and it will take a while for your skin to tan." She paused for a moment and then pulled off the towel covering her swimsuit. "Come on! Last one in is the hairy slug!" Caught by her enthusiasm and a massive surge of relief about not taking off his clothes, Wesley shambled towards the river. The water was deliciously cool as it lapped over his feet and ankles, but he found the mud squeezing between his toes unnerving, largely because he could not see his feet due to his tummy being in the way. Slowly, he shuffled in, so that the water streamed around his knees. He stood for a long time feeling the swirling brown liquid cooling his legs. He had decided that he did not want to go any further when he was hit by a massive spray of water. Isla, Freddie and Thomas had snuck back from the other side and were now pounding Anna and Wesley with spray.

"You rotters!" roared Anna, who promptly retaliated with great splashes of water. Freddie fired a large handful of mud at her back, which began to drip down inside her swimsuit. Anna spun around, tackled him and dangled his skinny body upside down over the water, as he squealed with delight. She dropped him swiftly into the churning river as the other two children came to Freddie's rescue. Soon, the river was a mass of tumbling limbs, water spray and flying mud.

Wesley stood slack-jawed at the edge of the action. He'd never seen a mother play with children like this. He could not remember the last time his mother had played with him at all. She would have certainly gone loopy if he had thrown mud down her underwear. He suddenly became aware that all had become quiet. The mother and children were lined up in front of him, up to their waists in water, united by a new enemy. With a great whoop from Freddie, Wesley was hit by a barrage of water. It seemed shockingly cold initially, as it swept over his hot skin. Scrabbling about in the water in an attempt to fight back, Wesley's fingers grasped great handfuls of mud. Without thinking, he hurled them across the river towards his assailants, and then more and more, smattering his companions with river silt. Suddenly, Freddie and Thomas were upon him, dragging him by the arms into the deeper water and soon his feet left the ground and he was swimming. The swirling brown water swept around him, revitalising, washing away the sweat of the morning.

"You'll need to swim slightly upstream as you cross the main channel," called Isla. "Follow me!" Wesley suddenly realised that he was now in fast-flowing water. He had told Anna he could swim, which was only partially true. He was very good at just bobbing about in a swimming pool, but he had never actually tried to go anywhere at speed. He felt the panic rise as the current began to catch him.

"You'll have to go for it," called Anna, who was just downstream from him. "Head for the bank swimming diagonally like Isla. Go on! It's not far. Swim!" Wesley started to flap his limbs frantically in the water, propelling himself forward. He could feel the current sweeping him away. He wasn't going to make it. He could feel himself gasping for air. The power of the water was relentless. His muscles were aching with the effort when he abruptly felt the water pressure ease. He was in an eddy on the far side of the main channel. His wild, flapping kicks were now carrying him easily towards the bank. He hauled himself on to the mud, wheezing and panting, groggy with fear. Two faces appeared before him, strange barbaric faces, mud caked in their hair and dripping from their eyebrows. Both wore enormous grins.

"Good effort," laughed Anna. "I thought you were going to end up as crocodile food in Samburu for a moment."

"And you're a pretty good shot with a mud pie if Mum's face is anything to go by!" added Isla gleefully.

The shade of the acacia tree was badly needed by noon. They lounged on picnic rugs enjoying a feast of egg sandwiches, chopped carrots, watermelon and little mango and pineapple pies that Anna had cooked the night before. Wesley was exhausted and starving but found himself smiling when he thought about the morning. He won at cards after lunch and was chuffed when Isla pointed out how quickly he had learnt the rules. Freddie and Thomas went back to the water's edge to hunt for lizards that sunned themselves on the hot rocks by the river. The others remained companionably in the shade. Wesley lay on his back staring through the branches of the acacia tree, with its menacing thorns. Clear blue sky glittered beyond, with small, creamy clouds gradually building up in the afternoon heat. He broke the silence.

"You know, you're not at all like my mum," he said to Anna. She put down the magazine she had been flicking through and tilted her head on one side.

"What was she like?"

Wesley did not know how to respond.

"Oh, just Mum really." His mum had just been there, and he had accepted her and his life without question. He had not thought about how other families might be different until he met Anna. Isla and Anna waited in silence; after a while, he continued. "I've spent nearly all my life with her. She was always just there. The person I did everything with." He smiled. "She really enjoyed watching medical dramas on TV, so we became experts at diagnosing people and doing first aid." He sighed sadly. "Well, we never actually had to help anyone, because we didn't go out much, but I know all about giving mouth-to-mouth and getting people breathing again and everything." Wesley was silent for a long time.

Eventually, Anna said gently, "Wesley, what happened in the end?"

In the speckled shade of the acacia tree, Wesley began to talk – haltingly at first and then with more confidence, as he allowed his mind to return to Yorkshire, to his mother, to his life, to the horror and despair.

Anna and Isla waited in silence as hot, angry tears coursed down Wesley's cheeks.

"How can I call a man I've never met before 'Dad'? He's done nothing fatherly in his whole life. He didn't know I existed a few weeks ago and now he wants to boss me around and put me on a diet!" He finished his tale with a furious splutter. "It's not fair! I don't want to be me! Why can't I be like Simon?" Anna quickly brushed the tears from her eyes and let Wesley's sobbing subside, while Isla offered him the nearest towel with which to wipe his eyes and blow his nose.

Finally, Anna spoke, "Wesley, I'm so sorry. I would have never brought you swimming if I had known." Wesley blew his nose on the towel again and gave her a lopsided smile.

"Actually," he said through the tears, "this is the most fun I've had for months."

"Well, I suppose it has been a pretty good morning," agreed Anna. She thought for a while, chewing her lip. "Wesley, there are some things that we can't change. Nothing will bring your mum back, but . . ." She took a deep breath. "You do have the power to change your life and achieve what you want to achieve. If there was one thing you wanted to change, what would it be?"

Wesley stared down at the river where the two boys were hopping from rock to rock and talking animatedly in excited bursts. He had never really had a friend. He had rarely joined in other children's games. He wasn't able to keep up in games of tag; he couldn't climb the tree they used as a den. He could not interest others in what he had done at the weekend because he never did anything of interest. He knew from the looks in their eyes that the other children at school judged him, thinking he was greedy and lazy, even though they never actually spoke about it.

He finally looked up at Anna. "I want to be able to join in, have friends and play with other children," he decided.

"And what is stopping you from doing that at the moment?" she replied. Wesley stared down at the grass, twisting the snotty towel in his hands. He hated to admit it, but he already knew the answer. Eventually, he looked up and met her gaze.

"I don't want to be fat anymore."

Anna nodded thoughtfully. "People come in all sorts of shapes and sizes, and we should celebrate that wonderful variety. It is OK to be different," she said simply. "But if your weight is affecting your health and holding you back from being the kind of person that you want to be, then it has become a problem."

"I know," he replied quietly. "It's a big problem and something that I'd like to change."

"Good," she said. "That sounds like the beginning of a plan."

Any further conversation was abruptly cut short. Anna instantly became tense and alert.

"Freddie! Thomas! Here, now! Move slowly," she commanded. "Isla, the picnic. Wesley, get in the car now!" Wesley sat befuddled as the other children began to move swiftly towards the car. "Now, Wesley!" hissed Anna.

Wesley finally squashed himself into the passenger seat as the large bull elephant reached the water. He drank deeply and then began to play with the water, sending plumes of spray across the river. The elephant waded deeper, enjoying the cool touch of the water on his stomach, before slowly emerging on the sandy bank in front of the car. He pawed the ground menacingly, sending up a shroud of dust. Anna kept her hand on the ignition, ready to start the car if necessary. But the elephant was more interested in pouring a shower of dust over his wet flanks. He lumbered up the riverbank, within three feet of the car, paused to have a good scratch against a dead tree and slowly moved away into the bush.

Everyone in the car started breathing normally again.

Freddie was the first to speak. "He was MASSIVE!" he exclaimed.

"Stunning," agreed Anna, slowly unwrapping the towel she had hastily draped around herself, over her swimsuit.

"He was tremendous," breathed Wesley, still straining to catch a last glimpse of the elephant as it disappeared from sight.

"Right. I think that is quite enough excitement for one day," stated Anna, turning to address the children in the back of the car. "Time to hit the road."

"Eewgh!" observed Freddie, "What's that gunge down your cleavage?" Anna looked down in dismay at the towel she had grabbed in the hurry to get into the car.

"Charming," she said. "I seem to be wearing Wesley's snot." Wesley looked horrified, but the others hooted with laughter. Anna winked at him.

"It could be worse. What are a few bogies between friends?" She smiled, "At least it's not elephant snot! Now that would be impressive!"

Henry Foster dropped his rucksack just inside the front hall. A fine cloud of sandy dust billowed away from it and settled among the pile of shoes and school bags by the kitchen door.

"Hi there. You're later than usual," called Anna, looking up from her computer. "Did it all go according to plan?"

"Pretty good, considering we were training a thousand soldiers," replied Henry. "Only one snake bite, two scorpion stings, a sprained ankle and one soldier wounded by an elephant." Anna glanced up again.

"Ouch, that must have hurt. How on earth did that happen?"

"Long story, but he was lucky not to be trampled to death," replied her husband. "The medics did a good job in flying him to Nairobi so quickly. It just shows that you can't be too careful with elephants." He leant over the sofa and planted a dusty kiss on the back of her neck, glancing at her computer screen in the process. "What are you looking at?"

"I'm searching for information on childhood obesity."

"Humph, it's pretty straightforward," Henry scoffed, subsiding in an exhausted heap on to the sofa. "Eat less and exercise more. Problem solved."

"That's easy for you to say. You come from a family which is naturally skinny. Some people are genetically much more susceptible to gaining weight than others. Anyway, it's a little more complicated than that," corrected Anna, going back to the webpage.

"Is this about Sergeant Mac's boy? How did the picnic go?"

"I thought it was going to be hard work, but surprisingly it went rather well," she replied. "And it got me thinking about how a child can become so desperately overweight. So, I've been doing some research."

"And what makes obesity complicated?" asked Henry, wearily taking off his boots.

"Well, I tended to think that people who are overweight must be doing the wrong thing, like eating too much and not taking enough exercise. But the data shows that actually our lifestyles over the last fifty years have changed so much that everyone is in danger of being overweight, unless we actively do something to prevent it. For many people, it has become normal to eat lots of processed food which is full of sugar and refined carbohydrates." Henry did not interrupt her, so she continued. "You see, our bodies have evolved to cope with surviving when food is scarce, and the norm was to have to work hard physically just to gather enough food to eat. Whereas now, in Western societies, there is high-energy food available everywhere and many of our jobs and lives require almost no physical effort at all. Did you know that over sixty per cent of adults in the UK are overweight or obese? That is more than half the population, which means that about half the children in the UK will be growing up with overweight parents as role models."

Henry looked up from peeling off his socks. "Sixty per cent?" he echoed "I didn't know it was that much." He paused. "But Wesley must have been a complete couch potato to get as huge as he is. He is more than just overweight."

"Yes, I agree. He and his mother made some bad decisions, but the interesting thing to look at is *why* she made those decisions. If you start from the point that we are all at risk of being overweight, you can see that it does not take much for things to start going downhill. Do you remember when you injured your back a couple of years ago?"

"Yes. I gained five kilograms in two months. Gosh! I'd forgotten about that."

"And it took you over six months and a lot of effort to get back to your normal weight again. And that was despite doing a job where you are given time to exercise each day. Most people have to find time to exercise outside work, which can be tricky if you have children to look after."

"Hmm," grunted Henry, examining the grime between his toes. Anna ploughed on.

"Things can go wrong for all sorts of reasons – for example, when people become isolated from their friends and family, are bereaved, go through divorce, become depressed, perhaps lose their jobs or have an injury. People may eat lots of processed food without realising the negative effect it can have on the body, particularly as the packaging often implies that it is healthy. Because there is so much fast food and ready meals available, many people have never been taught how to cook. Suddenly, they find they have gone from overweight to seriously overweight and it is more difficult to take exercise. Getting life back under control seems like an impossible task. What you must remember about childhood obesity is that it is the *adults'* decisions that usually lead to children being overweight." Anna continued, enthused by her new knowledge. "Once overweight, children are at risk of all kinds of other problems, such as low self-esteem, bullying, not doing well at school, being less popular and so on, which makes them more likely to turn to comfort eating. The weird thing is that parents of obese children often don't perceive them as being obese. The parents are so used to their children being overweight that they don't see it as a problem; it just becomes normal."

"There is nothing normal about Wesley!" joked Henry.

"I agree," said Anna, suddenly serious. "Henry, when you saw Wesley for the first time, what did you think of him? I mean what assumptions did you make about the kind of person he is?"

"Honest answer?" replied Henry. Anna nodded. "Well, the only thing I really noticed was how big he was, and I suppose if I'm really honest, I assumed that he must be greedy, lazy and have no self-discipline. Not a very politically correct reaction, I'm afraid."

"No, but from what the research says, it is a typical reaction," she replied. "Imagine how you would feel if people assumed that you were lazy and selfish whenever they first met you."

"I'd be gutted," admitted Henry quietly. "You'd always be fighting an uphill battle to prove you were worthwhile."

"Exactly," Anna agreed. "I think most people are aware of the physical health problems associated with obesity, but I'd never really looked into the psychological side of it," she said.

Henry pondered for a moment. "It's odd," he mused. "How obesity is a serious, avoidable problem that affects thousands of people and yet talking about it feels so awkward. It seems wrong to comment about someone else's body or appearance, even though we all secretly make judgements about people, based on how they look."

"Yes, I know. Also, we are so used to seeing overweight people that it has almost become normal. Imagine if over half the population had a terrible skin disease that cost the NHS billions of pounds to treat each year and was usually avoidable by changing their habits. I think it would be a different case. You would change your behaviour if your child was covered in nasty purple spots."

"My son is usually so covered in mud that I don't think anyone would notice if he had spots," laughed Henry.

Anna smiled but became thoughtful again. "Wesley's had a pretty difficult life up until now, and I'm not sure that Pete is going to cope. What Wesley needs most is friends and good role models. People who are going to support him, so that he can feel happier, lose weight and get back to a healthy lifestyle."

"And you feel that you are the woman for the job," Henry grinned.

"Well, I'd like to try. I'm going to help him, Henry," said Anna determinedly. "I'm going to find a way to help him and to help Pete. Wesley deserves a second chance." Henry put his hand on her knee.

"My love, I know better than to dissuade you when you have a plan," he said. "And for what it's worth, I think it is a good plan. If you can find a way to help, go for it." He leant forward and kissed her fondly, wafting a stench of dried sweat and African dust in her direction.

"Thank you for your support," she said, grimacing. "Now, please go and shower. You are absolutely honking."

"I've been living in the bush for ten days and driving in thirty-degree heat on dirt tracks for the last eight hours. Not to mention spending an hour under the bonnet of my wagon changing the radiator hose. What do you expect?" he challenged.

"I expect this great smelly monster to get into the shower," she said, pushing him in the direction of the stairs.

"OK, OK," he submitted.

"Supper in ten minutes," she called after him, sighing when she spotted the large oily handprint he'd left on her thigh. A distant thumping of feet came from upstairs, followed by delighted squeaks and excited chatter. "You're supposed to be asleep!" Anna shouted up the stairs, trying to keep the amusement out of her voice. Freddie's face appeared over the banisters.

"We can't sleep, there's a daddy in the house!" he squealed, before bouncing back towards the main bedroom. Isla emerged on to the landing, smiling.

"It's lovely to have him back," she grinned.

"Yes. It is," her mother agreed. But Anna considered revising her opinion when she saw the two grimy handprints on the back of Isla's pink pyjamas.

"Hmm. Next time, I'm going to hose him down before he gets through the front door," Anna resolved.

Chapter Four

"I'm not sure this is a good idea," complained Wesley, as they set off down the dirt track in the early morning.

"Well, you have to start somewhere, and you agreed that walking to school would be a sensible place to start," replied Isla cheerily. Wesley remembered walking the fifty metres around the corner to his school in the UK. Walking three kilometres each way was a much more daunting prospect. He wobbled down the uneven surface after Freddie, who was skipping in speedy zig-zags across the track.

On the first morning, they were twenty-five minutes late for school. Isla had tried not to look frustrated by Wesley's slow progress, but she could not believe it was possible to walk so slowly. Wesley remembered nothing about the journey, apart from the misery. His thighs chafed against each other as he walked, his feet were sore, he panted, huffed and puffed, and he was dripping with sweat by the time he staggered into the classroom.

"Sorry we're late, Mrs Wambui," apologised Anna, sticking her head around the classroom door. "My fault; we were late setting off." The class observed the state of Wesley and doubted very much that the family's lateness was anything to do with Isla's mother.

Wesley spent the morning in a daze. Once he had recovered his breath, he felt an overwhelming desire to go to sleep, which did not help his concentration in maths. However, this was soon replaced by a desperate, gnawing hunger, which the fruit at break time did nothing to alleviate.

DOI: 10.4324/9781003207986-5

The plan had been for them to walk home as well, but Anna was there in the car at the end of the day.

"Why the change of plan?" questioned Freddie. Anna watched Wesley hobbling out of the classroom. "I think we need to take this one step at a time," she replied. "It is uphill most of the way home."

The routine continued for the rest of the week, except that they left half an hour earlier, which meant getting up even earlier. Wesley felt totally exhausted. Almost every part of his body was complaining. His dad was being really fierce about "healthy eating" and Wesley had been desperately craving comfort foods all week. He didn't know how Pete could think that dry chicken and soggy vegetables were healthy. School lunches weren't much better.

"What on earth is this?" he'd asked Isla on the first day, pointing at a pair of godforsaken East African vegetables lurking on his plate.

"That's ugali. It's a paste made out of maize flour. It doesn't taste of much but does tend to stick to the roof of your mouth." Isla explained. "And the green one is skumerwiki, I think it is a type of kale cooked with lots of salt." Wesley examined the cream-coloured slop and its malevolent dark-green companion and pushed the plate away in disgust. He thought longingly of the crisps, pizzas and packs of mini-rolls that he and his mother would eat in front of the television on a Saturday night.

On Friday morning, Wesley flopped down at his desk in the classroom, feeling desperately low. He dreadfully missed his mum, he missed his flat, he missed UK TV, UK food – in fact, everything about the UK. Most of all, he could not bear being hungry anymore.

Oblivious to Wesley's desolation, Mrs Wambui began to address the class. "Now, I know it is a long time in the future, but we need to plan the Year Six end-of-year trip. You will all be transferring to different schools in September, and it would be great to have a really special outing, which you would all remember when you leave here. There is some money that we have put aside to fund a trip and I have some ideas of good activities, but I wanted to see if you had any suggestions." There was a buzz of excitement from around the room as ideas began pouring out.

"Let's go to Ol Pejeta on a game drive."

"How about swimming in the waterfalls in the Ngare Ndare Forest?"

"Can we go camping, Mrs Wambui?"

Through the thronging opinions, one voice spoke clearly, arresting everyone's attention.

"I think we should climb Mount Kenya," suggested Simon. The idea was immediately seized upon by the rest of the class.

"What an awesome idea!"

"We could camp by Lake Michaelson."

"I'd like to see the dawn rise at the top."

Mrs Wambui cleared her throat. "Thank you, everyone. Climbing the mountain is a super idea, Simon, but we must remember that it is a very strenuous climb. It may be a bit ambitious for you to do this year." Unintentionally, her eyes moved over Wesley as she said this. The rest of the class took in his massive, sweating frame, and the reality slowly dawned on them that if Wesley was to join them on the trip, there was no way they would be climbing Mount Kenya. Mrs Wambui rushed on. "You have had some great ideas, which I've jotted down. I'll speak to Miss Omwoto and we'll discuss the best options. Right, can you all get out your English books, please?"

Wesley was aware of the tension in the air throughout the morning. No one said anything, but it was quite clear that the rest of the class were united in wanting to climb the mountain and would not be allowed to because of him. He initially thought that the best thing was to just tell them to go without him. But as the morning continued, he began to burn with resentment about why everyone else always had all the fun. His anger began to focus on Simon who had suggested the trip. *Simon probably proposed it just so that I would be left out*, seethed Wesley. Simon was always leaving him out, going off and playing football each break time, doing backflips and cartwheels across the playground between lessons. Simon had deliberately suggested climbing Mount Kenya just to make him look pathetic, Wesley decided. By break time, Wesley was a boiling cauldron of bitterness.

When the bell went for break, the class streamed out of the classroom with Wesley lumbering in their wake. Simon's peg was next to the door and he was bent over trying to reach a book from the bottom of his rucksack when Wesley caught his toe in one of the rucksack straps. With a massive 'Whump!', Wesley sprawled on the paving outside the classroom. His arms had not broken his fall and the side of his face squashed into the ground. Rapidly, his classmates came to his rescue, voicing concern, picking up his bag, slowly helping him to his feet. Simon was at Wesley's elbow helping to lift his weight off the ground, careful not to brush the nasty graze that was already oozing blood on his elbow. Wesley slowly righted himself, panting through the shock of the fall. He noticed Simon holding his arm and ferociously threw him off, determined to blame Simon for all his misfortunes.

"You did that on purpose!" he spat at Simon, who was struggling to regain his balance from where Wesley had thrust him into the bushes.

"I did not," he replied, bewildered. "I'm sorry, I didn't mean to make you trip."

"Yes, you did," retorted Wesley. "You've tried to make me miserable since the day I arrived here. You and your smug backflips and your dad's fancy helicopter– you only do it to show off and make me feel pathetic." Simon appeared stunned by the ferocity of the attack and blushed red to the tops of his ears.

"It's nothing to do with you. I've always done backflips. I just like gymnastics."

"You want to leave me out. That's why you want to climb the mountain – because you think I won't be able to do it, so I can be left behind."

"That's not it at all. It's my dad . . ." Simon defended, but Wesley cut in.

"Well, you're wrong. I **can** climb that mountain," he said, gesticulating at the distant peak. "And I **will** climb that mountain. So you can't get rid of me that easily. I'll show the lot of you!" he bellowed, jabbing his finger at his nine peers, who were watching the exchange like ice sculptures, frozen in disbelief. With a sob, he shambled off out of sight around the end of the classroom.

"Crikey! Are you all right, Si?" asked Neil, putting his arm around his friend's shoulders.

"Yeah, I'm fine," Simon replied as Neil led him away across the playground. But Isla observed that Simon's hands were shaking and his skin was unnaturally white beneath his tan. As ever, Isla could not abandon a lost soul. She was always the one to pick up a crying toddler or bring home an injured bird. So she did not consider leaving Wesley to stew behind the classroom.

"Emma, can you get some fruit for him? I'll get Miss Bridgette and the first-aid box," she said.

Miss Bridgette bandaged Wesley's elbow and disinfected his cheek, tut-tutting like a fussing hen. Isla came to sit beside Wesley and offered him some pineapple and a tissue.

"Well, that was quite a show," she commented. Wesley glowered at her, chewing on the pineapple greedily.

"I'm going to do it," he announced. Isla studied him carefully.

"Wesley, do you know anything about climbing Mount Kenya?" He made no comment, so she ploughed on. "The summit is almost five thousand metres – that's nearly the same height as one of the Everest base camps. It is a five-day walk up and down, and people often don't make it because of the altitude. Dad says it is so cold up there that there is ice on the inside of the tent each night. Near the top, it is so cold that the air can't hold any moisture and the inside of your nose dries out." She glanced at him again. "Wesley, it is a really big climb for adults, let alone children." She brutally waved her hand over his body, "Let alone you."

She let the words hang between them, not daring to add anything else.

"I'm going to do it," he repeated, staring up at the peak. Isla sighed and smiled at the same time.

"In which case, you've got a very busy few months ahead, and Wesley . . ."

"Yeah."

"Go easy on Simon. You're not the only one with problems, you know."

Chapter Five

Wesley looked down in dismay at the blue floral apron that stretched across his girth.

"I don't think this is a very good idea," he grumbled.

"You always say that," retorted Isla, brandishing a wooden spoon. "Now, dry your eyes princess and get a hold of that fish!"

Wesley pouted and headed towards the pile of tilapia fillets on the chopping board. Anna's kitchen was unusually untidy. There were several rows of empty jam jars lined up on the side, and a huge vat of something khaki-coloured bubbling on the stove. Wesley sighed, looking at his apron again. "It's just not very manly, is it?"

"What's not manly?" asked Major Foster, emerging from the pantry with four jam jars between the fingers of his left hand. He was wearing a large pink apron stating "I LOVE JUSTIN BIEBER" over his army uniform. "What's not manly?" Isla's father asked again.

"Umm . . . cooking," mumbled Wesley.

"Cooking!" exclaimed Henry Foster. "Some of the best cooks in the world are men, including me!" He danced across the kitchen doing some nifty Scottish footwork and spun Isla in circles with his free hand. He deposited the jam jars on the side before raising his arms in a flamboyant French gesture. "*Regardez!* The best maker of runner bean chutney in the whole of Kenya!"

"Don't mind him," said Isla in a stage whisper. "He has problems with modesty."

DOI: 10.4324/9781003207986-6

"Yes! And with washing-up," complained Anna. "My feet stuck to the kitchen floor for a week after the last time you made chutney."

"Ah, but was it good chutney?" demanded her husband.

Anna relented. "Of course, you know it is always delicious."

"Aha! Just as I thought. Right, production line places, please, everyone. Freddie – get the jam funnel. Isla – you're in charge of labels. Chop chop, you lot. I've got to be back in the office in an hour." Wesley watched in fascination as the three of them poured, sealed and labelled thirty-two jars of chutney. Their instinctive teamwork was impressive, and even when it went wrong and Freddie poured boiling brown liquid across his father's hand, there were few cross words. Just profuse apologies from the boy, cold water on the hand and a raised eyebrow from the father, which very clearly said, *Watch what you're doing you little scoundrel, that REALLY hurt.*

"Right, Wesley, let's get on with this fish," said Anna, bringing him back to the task in hand. "As you can see, the new potatoes are already clean, so they can just be rolled in a little oil, salt and pepper and put on a tray to bake in the oven. While they are cooking, you can prepare the green beans. Then the garlic will go in the pan with a little butter and oil, followed by the fish. We can chop some mango and pineapple for pudding, while the rest of it is cooking. The whole meal should take no more than forty minutes from start to end." Wesley nodded and set to work on rolling the potatoes in a light film of oil. As he worked, his mind wandered back over the previous couple of months.

His decision to climb Mount Kenya had changed everything. The story of his outburst at Simon had raced around the school like a bushfire. Soon, every child and teacher knew about it and had something to say about the incident. To begin with, people had laughed. There was no way Wesley would make it up the mountain, they said. Then there was a wave of support for his effort. Soon people were clapping him on the back and congratulating him for such a gutsy decision. Miss Omwoto had said that she was impressed by his determination, and as everyone in Year 6 was so keen to climb Mount Kenya, she was happy to arrange and support the trip.

Anna had looked genuinely worried when Wesley and Isla had told her, but she kept her misgivings to herself and said they ought to make a "Mount Kenya Plan". Wesley had realised that Anna was always making plans. The first three weeks had been terrible. The walk to school continued to be awful, but now had the added pressure of knowing that everyone expected him to walk for five days up and down Mount Kenya. He continued to feel hungry all the time, and his dad's cooking was still virtually inedible. The exercise and the hunger made him feel exhausted, which in turn made him homesick and irritable.

It was at some point in week four that Wesley began to see a difference. He started to notice his surroundings on the walk to school. His thighs did not chafe as he walked anymore. He actually enjoyed the path that led down to the river and liked to pause on the rickety wooden footbridge, watching the river race over the stones that lined her bed. Usually, she was sparklingly clear and bitterly cold, having flowed straight off the slopes of the mountain. But if it had rained the day before, the river rose. Swollen with swirling red silt, she was a completely different creature compared with the sparkling goddess that usually sang and danced beneath the bridge.

The short hill that led up from the riverbank still made him pant, but he found that he recovered faster than he used to and was not sodden with sweat when he arrived at school.

Anna had talked him into walking home from school as well, which had initially been a terrible ordeal. The homeward journey was mainly uphill and much hotter than the crisp, cool air of the early morning. Wesley had cried on his first attempt and refused to go any further. His great, wailing sobs had amused the local children, who all gathered around, pointing at him and calling, "Howareyou? Howareyou?" as if the phrase was all one word. Anna had coaxed, cajoled, threatened and pleaded with him to continue, but Wesley had refused to budge. Eventually, she flagged down a passing donkey cart and Wesley rattled his way home among a load of bricks. As he sat sniffing in the brick dust, he looked ahead, watching the mountain peaks emerge from a carpet of cloud. They stared at him with bleak, jagged eyes, as if mocking him for daring to say that he, fat Wesley, would conquer the mighty mountain. Wesley groaned and looked away from the mountain to the back of the cart. To complete his humiliation, he saw all the Fosters and the cart driver pushing the cart up the hill to ease the donkey's load. "You're pathetic," he muttered to himself.

His second attempt to walk home had been slightly more successful, in that he had made it home, but only through grim determination, shuffling each foot painfully forward. As he ploughed up the hill, his lungs burned, gasping in great breaths, which did not satisfy him. Anna explained that it was the altitude. Nanyuki lies at nearly two thousand metres above sea level and so the air is much thinner than in the UK. This meant that until Wesley acclimatised properly, he would be even more breathless than normal. Despite the agony, Wesley had made it. He walked home from school twice a week, to begin with, gradually building up until he was walking to and from school daily, a round trip of six kilometres. That was something that filled Wesley with pride, and pride, he discovered, was an interesting and novel emotion. It took him by surprise because he had never felt proud before. He had never completed anything that had required sheer grit and determination. Although it had been a grim few weeks, Wesley was chuffed to bits.

The cooking had been another one of Anna's plans. Wesley had been whingeing yet again about Pete's awful cooking when she had remarked, "Well, Pete is pretty busy at work. Maybe it is time you learnt to cook."

Wesley was aghast. It wasn't his job to cook – he was only a child. Anyway, there didn't seem to be much food in the shops in Nanyuki that he felt was worth cooking. There was almost no processed food. Everything had to be cooked from scratch. He had no idea what to do with aubergines, broccoli, mangoes and great lumps of beef.

When Anna asked what meals he missed most, Wesley had replied without hesitating. "Pizza, chicken nuggets and fish and chips."

"OK. Well, it is hard to get good pizza here, so you will have to make your own. There is a place in town where we can buy pizza dough, which you can keep in the freezer. Then it is just a case of adding a nutritious topping, and I'm afraid you will have to have salad with it." Wesley scowled. "Don't worry, salad can be pretty good if it has a tasty dressing. So, let's start with pizza, then I'll show you how to cook chicken fillets, followed by fish," Anna concluded.

And that was how the cooking had started. Not every meal had been a triumph, and there had been quite a few charred pizzas until he got the hang of the oven. But

Wesley had to admit that he had actually enjoyed most of the meals he had cooked. The best thing about it was that Wesley was now able to teach Pete some recipes, and they were beginning to enjoy cooking together. This was a great improvement compared with their first few weeks when mealtimes had been a bitter battleground, which had often resulted in them both seething with anger and misery. On many nights, Wesley cried himself to sleep, while Pete drank too many beers alone downstairs.

Wesley looked across at Anna and smiled. Perhaps guardian angels really did exist, he thought. This woman might prove to be his saviour. He carried the tray of potatoes over to the oven and began trying to open the oven door with the tray in one hand. As he wrestled with the door, he became aware of an all-too-familiar feeling of sagging. His school shorts were starting to slip down his bottom, probably taking his pants with them. They had been doing it all week, usually at the most inconvenient times. Wesley frantically looked around for somewhere to put the potatoes, but all the kitchen surfaces seemed covered in jars of chutney. The tray was too hot to just dump on the side, and Anna had moved the chopping board it had been resting on a minute before. In a panic, he flung open the oven, aware that his shorts had crept several inches lower. He thrust the potatoes into the oven, as his shorts and pants came to rest around his knees. Isla's gasp behind him made it clear that she had been subjected to the sight of his huge, naked bottom. He wrenched his shorts back up and could feel his whole body blushing feverishly. He could not believe that he had just "mooned" the entire Foster family. He stood motionless, one hand clutching the oven door, the other holding up his shorts.

"Whoa! It's the Naked Chef!" chortled Henry Foster. "However, that's obviously good news. Judging by the speed at which those shorts came down, you must have lost weight." Freddie began snorting with laughter until he eventually curled up on the floor, clutching his sides. Anna was looking slightly stunned, a sharp knife in hand, raised like a guillotine over a pineapple. She put down the knife and came over to examine the waistband of his shorts. They were now several centimetres too big, whereas his belly had spilt over the top when he had first arrived. Without warning, she gave him a huge hug.

"Congratulations!" she cried. "You're losing weight. Oh, gosh, I suppose sewing lessons will be next. These shorts need taking in."

Wesley couldn't look them in the eye.

"My clothes have been getting a bit looser," he confessed. "Dad weighed me the other night and I've lost five kilograms. What's a bit depressing is that I feel I've lost a lot of weight, but no one else has noticed. I still look like 'the fat boy' to them."

Anna smiled encouragingly. "But, Wesley, five kilograms is a tremendous first step. By the time we get you up that mountain, you'll be as trim as a gazelle." Wesley returned a lopsided smile.

"Perhaps, but probably more like a pregnant zebra," he laughed.

"Either way," added Henry, "I'm going to order your father to buy you a belt. We can't have you alarming the good ladies of Nanyuki with that bottom again!"

Chapter Six

The trip to the Aberdares had been planned for the end of the spring term. Both Pete and Henry had a few days off work, and everyone agreed that if Wesley and Isla were going to attempt to climb Mount Kenya in June, they ought to try a serious high-altitude walk. A date was set for Pete, Wesley and the four Fosters to climb up Le Satima, the highest point in the Aberdare Mountains.

Wesley's progress had been impressive over the previous couple of months. He walked to and from school daily without crying or making everyone late. Mr Mwangi, the PE teacher, had encouraged him to start jogging. This had been a deeply unpleasant experience for Wesley, who could not remember ever running anywhere in his life. He set off around the school playing fields at a shambling shuffle with Mr Mwangi bouncing beside him, making encouraging noises. Within fifty metres, Wesley felt as though his chest would explode. He gasped for air but did not seem to be able to suck enough oxygen into his body. Running at altitude was obviously going to be challenging. Mr Mwangi became worried that Wesley might be about to collapse, so he suggested that they run fifty metres and then walk fifty metres and so on, for a lap of the school grounds.

That had been the beginning. After that, Wesley spent part of each lunch break plodding around the school fields. On the second day, Isla and Emma came with him, and the day after that Neil and one of the other Year 6 girls kept him company. Soon, the whole school seemed to

 DOI: 10.4324/9781003207986-7

want to support his efforts. By the end of the first week, Wesley was surrounded by two groups of five-year-olds, all arguing about who would be allowed to run with him. He glowed quietly within. He had never had anyone fighting over spending time with him before. He settled the matter by saying they could all come. The little crowd set off with Wesley shuffling in the middle and the others dashing around him, like the swarm of bees following Winnie the Pooh. By the third week, Wesley was managing two laps of the playing field, running all the way. The younger children had lost interest in going with him, as the novelty of running in break time wore off, but one of the Year 5 or Year 6 pupils would always emerge as he put on his trainers, chatting to him as he puffed around the field.

On the Friday of the third week, Wesley found Simon at his side. Simon had kept away from Wesley since the day of the argument. He had been civil but made no attempt to spend time with Wesley beyond what was necessary in class. So, on that Friday, Wesley was surprised to find Simon (barefoot as usual) standing beside him.

Wesley felt bad about the way he had treated Simon; he realised that he had been looking for someone to blame for his own problems. He wished he had had the guts to apologise, but he never found the right moment, and as time passed, it had seemed easier to say nothing more about the incident. But Wesley had watched Simon more closely. Isla's comment about Simon having problems too had made him curious. Simon was intelligent and found the classwork easy. He was popular with children of all ages. He had Neil as his best friend, who was loyal and kind. Simon was also extremely athletic and an excellent gymnast. He was tall, strong for his age – and from the way that the girls looked at him, it was obvious that he was going to be a good-looking teenager. Last of all, his family must be rich. No one poor arrived at school in a helicopter. Wesley was dumbfounded. How could Simon of all people have problems? He quizzed Isla about it, but she had simply replied that she didn't know the details and that it wasn't her story to tell.

So Wesley had had no option but to observe Simon closely, and it was then that he began to notice certain oddities. When Simon arrived at school in the morning, he always leapt from the helicopter as if he had been scalded. He walked away with hunched shoulders and never looked back or raised a hand in farewell. Wesley noticed that as the aircraft lifted off and disappeared over the trees, Simon's shoulders seemed to relax, as though a huge burden had been removed. *Perhaps he feels travel sick and doesn't like flying*, Wesley wondered.

Wesley had never heard Simon talk about home. Most of the class grumbled about their parents or the journey home, or talked about what they did at the weekend. Wesley had been delighted that he had been able to join in such conversations, now that he increasingly went on trips with Pete and so had something interesting to say. But Simon never mentioned his life outside school. He neither complained nor enthused about his time at home. Lastly, Wesley had noted that there were times when Simon went very quiet and seemed to experience a silent, unexpressed anxiety. It was usually when the class was given a test. Wesley could not understand why Simon might be anxious.

He always did better than anyone else and so had no reason to worry.

The two boys plodded around the sports pitches in silence. Wesley was unable to speak because he was panting so much. Simon seemed to have nothing to say, but the pair were comfortable in their own thoughts. It was towards the end of the second lap that Simon finally spoke.

"You know, I'm sorry if I haven't been very friendly towards you." He paused, picking his words carefully. "I suppose I didn't think we would have much in common. But I just wanted to say that I really admire you for getting fit. I can see how hard it has been for you, and losing your mum must have been awful. So I just wanted to say that I hope you stick at it because it would be great if we could all climb Mount Kenya together." Wesley stopped running and sagged in the shade of a flame tree. He wanted to reply but was too out of breath to talk. Simon stood awkwardly, not knowing where to look, so he turned to stare at the mountain. Wesley followed his gaze. It was easier to apologise when not actually looking at each other.

"It's me who should apologise," Wesley started, still breathing heavily. "I was jealous of you and tried to blame you for all my problems. I'm sorry I shouted at you." Wesley realised that the apology was about three months late, but now had been the right time and it felt good to have finally said sorry. Simon smiled and shrugged.

"No worries. I guess neither of us are perfect." Then, changing the tone, "Hurry up – you can't use a heart-to-heart chat as an excuse to not finish your run."

Wesley groaned and plodded after him.

Another two months had passed since the truce with Simon. On the first day of the Easter holidays, the party set off at dawn, bound for the Aberdare Mountains. The weather had been perilously dry since Christmas and the water shortages were really biting. Many families had been without running water for over a month. The grass and shrubby bushes were withered to crisp, browning shards in the merciless sun. Rivers were dry. Cattle, sheep and goats wandered listlessly on bony limbs, unable to chew any nutrition or moisture from the parched remnants of the grass. The weak and weary fell by the roadside and were unable to rise again.

Bushfires had sprung up everywhere, ravenously consuming any pathetic remains of vegetation, driven by winds that had started to bring billowing clouds over the mountain in the afternoons. The locals said that when the mountain burned, the rain would come. Stories circulated about people deliberately setting fires in the hope of encouraging the rains to start. And yet no rain had fallen. Hence, the fires raged and glowed on the mountain slopes in the night.

Henry Foster drove south from Nanyuki in the dreary light of dawn, with all six of them crammed into the Land Rover. He observed the cloudless sky, as the sun began to rise cautiously behind Mount Kenya.

"We picked a good day for it," he noted. "I reckon the rains will break within a few days. It's good we didn't leave this trip any later."

"How high is Le Satima, Sir?" asked Pete from the back.

"I think it is pretty much exactly four thousand metres. So, we shouldn't be at risk of altitude sickness, but we will certainly notice that the air is thin. The map shows that we can drive up to a saddle between two hills at about three thousand metres and walk from there. It should be easy to get up and down within a day."

"What happens when you get altitude sickness?" asked Freddie, evidently hoping that it would have a range of gruesome and undignified symptoms. Henry explained.

"The higher you climb, the thinner the air becomes. Our bodies are not used to coping with less oxygen in the air and so it is important to climb big mountains slowly, to give your body time to adjust."

"What happens if you climb it too quickly?" questioned Freddie.

"Some people are fine, but others feel ill, and it is frequently impossible to predict who will be affected. It often starts with a headache, feeling very tired and sick. It stops your brain working effectively, so people can become confused and disorientated. That means that they start making bad decisions, which can be serious when you are climbing a mountain."

"Can it kill you?" asked Isla, sounding worried.

"Not usually – if you are sensible. You need to listen to your body. If you start suffering, you need to come back down, and then people usually feel better pretty quickly. But it can be dangerous, sometimes deadly, particularly if you ignore the signs." Isla caught Wesley's eye, giving him an anxious look.

The vehicle turned off the main Nairobi road and bumped westwards towards the Aberdare National Park. They headed down a precipitous dirt track, which wound like a serpent into a steep valley and then up again. On either side, the jungle stretched in impenetrable swathes, with massive trees shading the track. Wesley peered out of the window, expecting Tarzan to come swinging through the foliage on a trailing vine. They met a stone track at the top of the valley and rattled steadily up through the forest. Gradually, the trees thinned and were replaced by huge bamboo plants, which stood like ranks of silent soldiers, except in places where they had been brutally thrust aside by passing elephants.

The bamboo gave way to a rosewood forest, made of massive ancient trees with outstretched branches and mossy trunks. Trails of lichen draped the branches like mermaids' hair. They turned off the main marram track and on to a little-used dirt path. It had ruts so deep that the Land Rover began to scrape along the grass in the middle of the track and was in danger of grounding if the tyres sank further into the mud. Henry skilfully steered to the edge of the track so that one wheel ran along the edge of the path and the other on the ridge in the middle. However, where it was muddy, the vehicle sometimes slipped back into the ruts with a sickening lurch. Anna watched Henry concentrating, grim-faced, nursing the vehicle up the hill. As they progressed, the ruts became less deep and he gratefully let the wheels sink into them, aware of the sheer drop that had emerged on the right. In fact, the track was little more than a ledge, cut into the side of the mountain.

"They've had rain up here. This track could get interesting if it rains before we get back down," he warned. Anna nodded, all too aware that when Henry described a road as being "interesting", she usually found it life-threatening. Suddenly, to her relief, the track turned away from the precipice and continued up, out of the trees and into a rugged moorland landscape.

"Oh! We've arrived in Scotland," announced Freddie. Henry laughed.

"Yes, you would never imagine that we are only just south of the equator. It's not far now. The car park is in the dip between those hills," he said, pointing out of the driver's window.

When Major Foster mentioned a car park, Wesley had imagined a neat tarmac area with white lines demarcating the parking spaces, and probably a pay-and-display machine to one side. So he was surprised when the Land Rover rose over the crest of the slope and stopped on an open piece of ground, nestling between two hills. There was no sign of any cars or any type of human habitation, just miles and miles of rolling moorland. If something went wrong up here, thought Wesley nervously, they were going to be in real trouble.

Chapter Seven

The first two hours of walking passed without incident. Henry set a slow pace so that they could cope with the altitude. Freddie cantered ahead, occasionally stopping to catch a startled frog or some unfortunate invertebrate. Wesley found he was almost enjoying himself. The sun was shining, and the air was so fresh and cool it felt as though it was washing his lungs with each breath. He had lost a considerable amount of weight in recent months, and he felt capable of taking his new slimmer body up the hill.

They stopped for slabs of banana cake, nuts, raisins and water. When they set off again, Wesley suddenly felt tired. His legs were heavy. His new walking boots rubbed his toes. His eyes ached against the dazzle of the morning sun. He began to whinge, a never-ending stream of niggles, moans and complaints.

"Are we nearly there yet? . . . My boots are too tight . . . My knee hurts . . . Can I have a rest? . . . I need some water . . . I need a biscuit . . . The biscuit's made me thirsty . . . How much further? . . . I need another rest . . . My feet hurt . . . What's that noise? . . . I think something is following us; we need to turn back." And so on.

Anna responded to the last statement. She had heard the noise, too. It was an eerie rattling sound that seemed to follow them up the mountainside. She scanned the hillside, looking for danger, aware that even at this height buffalo might be around. The wind gusted across the hillside, and the ominous rattling sounded again.

DOI: 10.4324/9781003207986-8

"Aha! Caught in the act!" accused Anna. "That's the culprit. It is the wind rattling the dead leaves of the giant lobelias."

"What on earth is 'a giant earlobe'?" muttered Wesley moodily.

"Giant lobelia," corrected Anna. "Look, they are the tall plants over there. As the plant grows, the dead leaves stay attached and make that awful rattling noise in the wind. Ooof, they somehow remind me of triffids".

"What are triffids?" asked Isla.

"Triffids, now that's a fascinating story by a man called John Wyndham," replied her father. He began to tell the tale of *The Day of the Triffids*. He explained about the main character in the book, a biologist who worked with triffids – nasty venomous plants, which could move around on strange root-like legs. Worst of all, the plants were aggressive and ate meat. Henry explained the plague of blindness that swept the world when people's eyes were damaged by watching a meteor shower, and then how the triffids began to overrun the country.

The children listened, completely absorbed by the story, as they traversed the ridgeline over a knoll and towards the final ascent. They peppered him with questions about triffid behaviours and about how humans could survive if they were blind. Each time the wind blew, the lobelia leaves gave their deathly rattle, which made the children shriek with delight as Henry made the plants seem as gory and fearsome as possible.

Wesley forgot about his sore feet and legs, allowing his imagination to soar on the details of the story, and so he was surprised when Pete said, "Right, nearly there. Dig in for the last climb everyone."

The last section was more of a scramble than a walk, straight up the steep side of the summit. Wesley was not used to scrambling up rough, rocky ground and found it both nerve-wracking and exhausting. It took so much energy, having to decide where to put each foot. But he followed the Fosters and knew that Pete was right behind him, to break his fall if he slipped. He pulled, heaved, gasped and tripped up the final hundred metres and finally emerged, dazed and sweating, on to a small plateau on the crest of the hill. He slumped with his hands on his knees, trying to suck oxygen out of the thin air. The others were strangely silent and he looked up to see them with their arms draped around each other, staring at the view.

To the north and west, the Great Rift Valley stretched away, wrenched into a deep gulley by the ancient shifting of tectonic plates. It ran for hundreds of miles, littered with lakes at its depths, right up to Lake Turkana in the northern Kenyan desert and on beyond into Ethiopia. To the east, Mount Kenya was just visible through an increasing duvet of cloud, and the Aberdare Mountain Range stretched to the south with great rolling, undulating expanses of grassland on the hilltops, dropping down to forests below. Wesley was spellbound. He had never seen a view so impressive. He looked back down along the path that they had climbed, which seemed to stretch away for ever into the distance. *I did this!* he crowed silently to himself. *I have actually climbed a mountain!*

Pete stood behind him and put his hands on Wesley's shoulders.

"Good effort," he said quietly, as they both regained their breath. "It was worth the climb." Wesley smiled over his shoulder at his father and nodded wordlessly.

Freddie broke the spell. "I'm starving. What's for lunch?"

"Honestly, do you think of nothing else?" exclaimed his father. "I'm sure you've got worms."

"Oooh. I hope so," replied Freddie. "If they come out in my poo, can I keep them as pets?"

"Freddie, don't be disgusting," scolded his mother. "Here, have a sandwich." Anna sat down while rummaging for sandwiches to feed the children. They all chatted happily about the climb and what they would tell their friends on Monday. Anna soon noticed that the seat of her trousers was going soggy.

"Gosh, it's very wet up here, considering we are at the top of a mountain," she observed. "And what is that awful smell?" She stood up to investigate only to find that she had been sitting on an enormous buffalo poo.

"Phew! You're going to have to walk at the back if you smell that bad going down," remarked Isla.

"Has it got worms?" asked Freddie, jumping up to inspect the poo. "I hope you haven't squashed them all."

"For goodness' sake, Freddie, stop going on about worms." Anna looked despairingly at her husband for moral support, but he was lying on his back with his hands behind his head, smirking to himself.

"What I don't understand," said Anna crossly, "is that the buffalo have miles and miles of countryside in which to eat and poo. Why on earth would one choose to scramble all the way up here just to have a poo?"

"I suspect he wanted to see the view," laughed Wesley.

"No, he was definitely trying to impress all the lady buffaloes," retorted Isla.

"Nope," said Henry. "He was completing his buffalo secret agent training and had to come up here to get a radio signal to contact his HQ. He must have paraglided off the top over there, to go on his next secret mission."

Freddie's eyes sparkled. "He's probably helping James Bond stop a cunning plot as we speak. But even secret agent buffaloes can have worms, right?" he added hopefully.

"Oh, shut up, you horrid boy," said Anna good-naturedly. "Now, let's get off this hill before that rain hits."

They all looked up to the east where huge billowing clouds were building and darkening by the minute.

"Hmm. I agree. Time to go," decided Henry.

For the first hour or so of the descent, the children were elated with their achievement. The gentle climb down the ridgeline was easy going and they chatted happily. By mid-afternoon, however, they were all flagging. Three times they rounded a corner in the track and expected to see the car waiting in the distance, but only saw the hills rolling ahead in a never-ending sea of green. The storm hit them at about three p.m. They quickly donned waterproofs but found they provided little protection, as the hail battered their heads under the thin plastic coverings. The wind buffeted them in all directions and forced scatterings of hail into their faces and down their necks. It was a rather dejected party that finally arrived back at the car. Wesley was physically and mentally exhausted. Despite all his running around the sports pitches, his stamina was much poorer than the others, who were all naturally fit. He had only managed to drive himself on because he knew that reaching the Land Rover was his only hope of warmth and shelter.

By the time they all squeezed into the vehicle, they were drenched and feeling frozen. The temperature outside had plummeted as soon as the storm had hit. Rain was bucketing down like thundering nails on the roof of the vehicle, making it hard for Henry to see clearly through the windscreen. He edged the car around and back down the way they had come. The track had almost disappeared, replaced by a tumbling torrent of water that carried the run-off down the rutted tyre tracks. As the rain intensified further, the water overwhelmed the capacity of the track and, in places, spouted off to the left over the precipitous hillside, creating temporary waterfalls. Henry was concentrating hard. The track had been difficult on the way up, but it was terrifying on the way down. Freddie, oblivious to the danger, began singing.

"I know a song that will get on your nerves, get on your nerves, get on your nerves." Anna whipped round to shout at him.

"Shut up, Freddie! Not now!" Wesley exchanged glances with Pete as the Land Rover continued its slithering slide down the hill. They had never heard Anna lose her temper before. It was clear that she was genuinely frightened.

At last, the track moved away from the precipice and everyone relaxed a little. A deluge of water continued to gush down the deep ruts. The Land Rover grounded only once when the tyres lost traction in the mud and she sat on her belly like a stranded tortoise. After half an hour of digging, Pete and Henry managed to drag it out using the winch attached to a nearby tree. It was bliss to reach the stone road again, which although bumpy was easily passable in the rain. They drove through the bamboo until they came to the dirt road that swung steeply down into the jungle, over the river and up the other side. Henry stopped the vehicle and examined the path carefully.

"What's up?" asked Anna nervously.

"We can't go this way. It is black cotton. There is no way I will be able to get the Land Rover around those hairpin bends, and if we slip over the edge, we will all be killed."

Wesley nudged Pete and asked quietly, "What's black cotton?"

"It's a type of soil made from clay, which is incredibly slippery when wet. Black cotton roads are often impassable in the rainy season." Everyone stared at the lethal track leading off to the right until Henry made a decision.

"I'm sorry, everyone, we have to find another way. We will have to continue towards Mweiga until we find a road that is less steep." The mood in the car was tense, cold and damp. Everyone was steaming, which clouded the windows, making it more difficult for Henry to see clearly against the persistent rain. They passed junctions with many small, steep tracks on either side. After about ten kilometres, they came to a junction where a well-made stone track forked away to the right towards Mweiga.

"What do you think, Mac?" called Henry from the front.

"Looks good to me, Sir," Pete replied, peering at the road from the rear of the vehicle.

Gingerly, Henry steered down the side road. It sloped gently down and seemed to be fairly well constructed. They continued for a further two or three kilometres when abruptly the road surface changed to black cotton. The wheels immediately began to crab across the track as the clay in the soil made it more slippery than black ice. Henry controlled the skid well but cursed under his breath. Anna grasped the handle on the dashboard in front of her in an attempt to steady her nerves. The car continued to slither down the road, as Henry fought to control it.

"Henry, we should we turn back," Anna hissed.

"We haven't got a hope of turning and getting back up this hill until the road dries," he said grimly. "So, the only way is forward."

Henry was a skilled driver and navigated the road fairly well considering the treacherous soil, which was why the accident seemed even more shocking when it happened.

They rounded a gentle bend in the track to see that the right-hand side of the road had collapsed completely, leaving a gaping cliff where the road had been. Anna gasped and clutched the dashboard tighter. Henry frantically steered away from the drop but was hampered by a deep gully on the left of the road. He somehow managed to steer along what remained of the road while everyone held their breath. For once, even Freddie was speechless and he grabbed Isla's arm.

Pete and Wesley braced themselves in the back of the vehicle, but Pete could see that they should make it safely past the danger point. Then, without warning, the earth beneath the driver's side of the vehicle disintegrated. With a hideous lurch, the Land Rover dropped off the road, landing heavily on its side before rolling again to crash on to the roof. Everyone was thrown to the right as the car rolled. It began raining rucksacks, binoculars, maps, water bottles and sandwiches, as any loose items were thrown around in chaos. Wesley was stunned and disorientated.

He found himself hanging upside down by his seatbelt. He could hear the engine roaring and then go silent. He began fumbling with the catch to release himself in a total panic when he felt Pete's arms on his shoulders.

"You're all right. We're all right. I've got you," his father said calmly. Wesley felt the flash of panic subside, although his heart continued to thunder in his chest. He heard Henry call from the front of the car.

"Don't undo your seatbelts, anyone. If you drop head first on to the roof, you could break your neck. Now, is everyone all right? Sergeant Mac, I can't see behind me. How is everyone back there?"

"We're OK, Sir. Freddie's got a gash on his head, but I think he's OK."

"Talk to me, Freddie!" demanded Henry.

"I'm fine, Dad, but I've got blood in my eyes."

"OK. Don't worry, it will just be a cut. I'll have a look at it in a minute."

The driver's side of the car was buried deep in the mud where the road had collapsed. Henry looked over at his wife who was still clutching the dashboard.

"Anna, we're going to have to get everyone out your side into the bushes. Does your window still work? Try to wind it down." Numbly, Anna reached for the handle to wind down the window. Everything seemed to be in the wrong place, now that the car was upside down. It was harder to turn than usual, but she gradually managed to wrench the window open.

"Good. Well done. Now, put your hands on the roof and push up. I'm going to try to release your seat belt and take some of your weight at the same time. Try to take your weight on your arms and curl forward as you hit the roof to protect your neck. Ready?"

Anna nodded, still unable to speak, but aware that the car was starting to fill with a stream of sludgy water and that she needed to get the children out fast.

Henry fiddled, trying to release her seat buckle and suddenly she landed with a thump on the car roof. She immediately started to wriggle out of the window, into the bushes. She sat puffing in the sodden foliage for a few seconds before lunging towards the rear window which Freddie was struggling to wind down. He had a nasty gash in his chin and the blood had run up his face giving him a confused, macabre look. Anna smiled at him, trying to ignore the gaping wound on his chin. She lay in the mud and reached in the window, so as to be at his head height.

"Isla, I'm going to take his weight and then I need you to undo his seatbelt. OK. Go!" Freddie landed with a thump, and Anna helped guide him out of the window, closely followed by Isla. She peered through to Pete and Wesley who were hanging from their seatbelts in the rear of the wagon.

"Pete, are you two OK in there?"

"Yes, we're fine," he replied. "I'm going to try to get Wesley out of his seat belt and see if he can crawl through to you." Anna stuck her head back in the front window to find Henry fighting with his seat belt.

"I can't lift enough weight off it for the buckle to release," he panted. "Can you reach my knife? I'll have to cut it." Anna found the knife in the glove compartment.

"I'll cut it," she said decisively. "You brace yourself for the fall." Cutting the seatbelt was harder than she had imagined, particularly as she was worried about cutting Henry when he fell, but at last Henry landed heavily on the roof in a splash of mud. He strained to wriggle out from behind the steering wheel, cursing his long legs, and finally struggled free and grabbed his handheld radio. He found Anna dragging Wesley through the rear window. It was a tight fit, but he finally emerged. Henry helped to cut Pete free who was also trapped by his seat belt.

The whole party felt a surge of relief once they were all free of the vehicle, which was rapidly filling with silty brown water.

"Phew! That was quite an end to the day!" Henry laughed grimly, quickly checking everyone over for injuries. Anna was already holding a handkerchief to Freddie's chin which was bleeding heavily. Pete wrestled with the back door of the Land Rover, but it was jammed shut. So he wriggled back in through the window to rescue some food, water and the first-aid kit. He quickly leaned in again to retrieve Anna's handbag, which contained her phone and house keys. Henry picked up the radio and switched it on.

"Zero. This is Zero Alpha. Over." They all held their breath in the silence, listening to the gentle rustle of static on the radio net.

Then an efficient male voice said, "Zero. Send. Over."

"Zero Alpha. We have been involved in a traffic accident and require assistance. We are approximately five kilometres north-west of Mweiga. I'll send a grid reference shortly. We have got all six pax out of the vehicle, but we will need vehicle recovery and transport for four pax back to Nanyuki. Over."

"Zero, roger. Is anyone injured? Over."

"Zero Alpha, no serious injuries, but the med centre should stand by to do some stitches to a facial wound."

Henry continued to relay information and directions. Anna sat trying to stem the bleeding to Freddie's chin. *Thank God for the Army, Thank God for the Army*, she thought again and again. In an area with almost no ambulance service, accidents often became fatal very quickly.

They sat huddled in the bushes. Isla found that she was shaking uncontrollably, but felt a little steadier when Wesley sat beside her and put his arm around her shoulders.

"That was a close one," he said, feeling surprisingly calm now that he was out of the vehicle. Isla continued to shake. "It was lucky that I've lost so much weight or I might not have got out through the window," he pondered, suddenly struck by the horror of being trapped in the vehicle as it filled with muddy water. Isla smiled weakly and nodded.

Henry finished on the radio and turned to address Pete. "Mac, there's no hope of recovering the wagon until the road dries, but I think we should get the children home. Can you stay with the vehicle while I walk Anna and the children to Mweiga? It's only about five K. A vehicle will pick them up from there and then I'll walk back to join you. I'll take the handheld radio with me. You will be able to use the vehicle radio over this distance." Pete nodded.

"That's fine, Sir. Can you bring us back some coffee?"

Henry laughed. "I'll see what I can do."

And so it was that two hours later Wesley found himself in the back of another Land Rover bumping his way back to Nanyuki. As they had walked away from the Aberdares, the rain stopped and they found that there had been no rain at all in Mweiga. The roads back to Nanyuki were as dry and shrivelled as they had been when they left in the early morning. All the foliage was gasping and longing for rain. The sun streamed through the open window, drying their sodden clothes with its generous rays. Anna was sitting next to him with her arm around Freddie, who had fallen asleep. She suddenly let out a great shuddering sob and began to cry. Wesley looked at her aghast.

"I thought we would be trapped," she sobbed. "I thought I might lose one of you." Her tears made clean channels through the mud on her cheeks, and her nose began to dribble. Wesley rubbed her shoulder reassuringly, and as he did not have a handkerchief, he wiped the sleeve of his shirt across her nose.

"There," he said. "What are a few bogies between friends? Now I'm wearing your snot, so that makes us quits." Anna looked confused for a second and then smiled, remembering the day by the river.

"Not quite," she said. "You haven't got it down your cleavage."

"I'm sure we can arrange that," laughed Wesley.

Wesley continued to rub Anna's shoulder as she cried. He looked down at his filthy, bruised limbs and was surprised to find that he still felt it had been a good day. He had conquered his first mountain. He had survived a disaster. He had been comforted by his dad. But most important of all, he had been able to offer comfort and support to Isla and Anna. He had constantly absorbed their kindness and help in recent months, and at last, for the first time, he had felt able to help them in return.

Yes! It was a good feeling. Today had certainly been a good day.

Chapter Eight

The meeting about climbing Mount Kenya was held in May. The ten Year 6 pupils gathered with their parents in the classroom to talk through the arrangements for the climb. Most of the parents knew each other and chatted warmly. Wesley was sad that Pete and Henry were not there, but they were away on an army exercise. Anna smiled and gave him a thumbs-up, just as Miss Omwoto called for quiet.

"Thank you, everyone, for coming to the meeting this morning. As you know, we are all very excited about the Year Six trip up Mount Kenya next month. I am sure you are all aware that Mount Kenya is a major challenge, even for adults."

"Oh, come on," scoffed a loud voice at the back of the room. "I climbed the mountain when I was only nine. Any idiot with guts can do it." Wesley looked round to see who had rudely interrupted the headteacher and noticed a tall, lean man lounging on Mrs Wambui's desk. From his vivid green eyes, blond hair and general good looks, it was obvious that the man was Simon's father. Simon was sitting away from him at the edge of the classroom, fiercely staring at the floor. Miss Omwoto swiftly recovered from the interruption.

"Well, Mr Morgan, you are blessed with very athletic genes," she said, which caused a ripple of laughter around the room. "I am sure that you were a very fit and strong nine-year-old. In any case, I am very proud that all the children in Year Six are going to attempt the climb." At this point, she glanced at Wesley and winked at him. Wesley felt a

 DOI: 10.4324/9781003207986-9

rush of pride and blushed. He enjoyed the sensation as Miss Omwoto continued to explain the plan for the trip and how the ten children would be accompanied by their class teacher, Mrs Wambui, and Mr Mwangi the PE teacher.

However, as he listened, Wesley became distracted by the feeling he was being watched. The hair prickled on the back of his neck, and he felt as though something unpleasant was drilling into his soul. Against his better judgement, he glanced behind him and was shocked to see Mr Morgan's green eyes staring at him in disgust. There was something about the man's face that was so hard and completely devoid of warmth. Flustered, Wesley turned away again.

"There will also be two professional guides with the group," Miss Omwoto continued, "and a number of porters to help carry the tents and food." Again, she was interrupted.

"Are they not even having to carry their own kit?" demanded Simon's father. "I had to carry all my own clothes and food when I climbed the mountain."

An edge of irritation crept into Miss Omwoto's voice as she continued. "On this occasion, I have decided that the children would be best carrying only emergency food and additional wet-weather gear," she said firmly. "We are luckily able to afford for the children to be accompanied by some very fit and strong porters, who have climbed the mountain many times and so are accustomed to the altitude."

The parents smiled and nodded in agreement. Various other aspects of the trip were covered, such as what kit the children should pack, when they would be collected and returned, and what the emergency arrangements would be if someone was ill or injured.

Throughout the talk, Wesley felt as though he was being X-rayed by Simon's father. He had no idea why the man was interested in him, but for some reason Mr Morgan seemed to loathe him.

There was an opportunity to ask questions, and various parents contributed to the discussion. When the meeting was about to draw to a close, Mr Morgan's grating voice fired into the room once more from the back. Wesley involuntarily turned to face the speaker.

"It is quite clear that there are some children in Year Six," he stated, staring straight at Wesley, "who are unlikely to be fit enough, strong enough or determined enough to get to the summit." He paused, still staring at Wesley to ensure that everyone understood about whom he was talking. Wesley blushed for a second time, but this time he was hit by a rush of humiliation rather than a glow of pride. Mr Morgan continued, "Can you reassure me that the stronger members won't be slowed down by children who are not up to it?" Anna stood up suddenly as if to say something, but Mr Mwangi cut in, speaking in his slow, calm voice.

"The guide will force us to walk slowly so that everyone has time to acclimatise. As you know, Mr Morgan, it is impossible to predict who in the party may be affected by altitude sickness. You will also know that fitter individuals can be the worst affected. If anyone feels unwell or is unable to continue, we have two guides, so that one party can be brought off the mountain without affecting the others." Mr Morgan grunted and slouched back against the classroom wall.

Miss Omwoto swiftly concluded the meeting. "Thank you very much for coming, everyone. Our tag rugby match is due to start in ten minutes; I do hope that you will all be able to stay and support our team." Wesley sat in silence, as people milled around the classroom. Simon's father had made it quite clear that he did not think Wesley was up to climbing Mount Kenya and would just ruin it for everyone else. He should let them go without him, he decided. They would all have a better trip without him. As if reading his mind, he felt Anna's hand on his shoulder.

"Don't you dare wimp out just because of that old dinosaur," she whispered. "I've never heard him say a nice word to anyone. Come and watch the rugby with me. We will see if we can shout louder than everyone else."

Wesley was massively slimmer and fitter than he had been six months earlier, but he had not yet been selected for the tag rugby team. He stood with Anna and other parents and children, cheering on his classmates as they battled on the pitch. The opposing team were fearsome and swiftly scored two tries. Simon was clearly the home team's star player. He never dropped the ball and he hurtled up the pitch at astonishing speed but was stopped from scoring by a wall of defence. He finally scored two tries before half-time, which meant the teams were even when they stopped for refreshments. Simon's father had stood alone on the touchline, roaring directions at his son. Mr Mwangi called his team together as soon as they came off the pitch, but Simon's father strode over to the huddle and pulled his son roughly away by the arm. Wesley could not hear the conversation clearly, but he watched Simon absorb a deluge of criticism and angry gestures. Mr Morgan repeatedly jabbed his index finger into Simon's chest, and when Simon looked at his shoes, his father grabbed his chin to raise the boy's face to meet his eyes.

It was at this point that Mr Mwangi intervened, insisting that Simon was needed for a team talk. In fact, he said little, allowing Simon to drink and eat thick slices of watermelon before commenting, "Simon. You're the best player on the pitch and you are doing a great job. Well done."

Simon smiled weakly and returned to the game. His father paced the touchline like an angry scorpion waiting to strike. Suddenly, Isla's comment about Simon having problems of his own made sense to Wesley. Simon's father was a bully.

Wesley unexpectedly acknowledged that Pete had been incredibly supportive over the last few months, even though the two of them had had little in common when Wesley had first arrived. There had been difficult times, but, on balance, Wesley had to conclude that his life was actually pretty good most of the time. He was happier now than he could remember, but admitting that to himself resulted in huge waves of guilt. Guilt that he was happier with Pete (whom he had only known for a few months) than with his mother, who had cared for him for eleven years. With the guilt came grief for the life he had left behind and for the woman who had been his sole companion and who now he would never see again. He missed her, he loved her, but he resented her for allowing him to become obese, for encouraging him to think of eating as a fun pastime. He hated her for never taking him anywhere or doing anything interesting with him. But he realised that these were wasted emotions. She had loved him as much as she could; she just was not able to love herself enough to stay alive for him. Wesley breathed deeply and raised his face to the bright Kenyan sun. He would never be slim; he had a stocky build like Pete. But Wesley's body shape had completely changed. He could wear swimming trunks without dreading showing his body in public. He had adventures at the weekends. He had a father who was fun, practical and caring, even if he was still a pretty awful cook. Best of all, Wesley had friends, and that was better than being allowed to eat a dozen packs of chocolate mini-rolls. He watched Simon's father scowling at the pitch and felt grateful that he did not have to go home to that angry face every night.

Wesley turned to Anna, "Poor Simon," he murmured.

"Yes. Poor Simon. That man is merciless. His heart has been burnt to a crisp in the midday sun," she replied.

Chapter Nine

Pete and the Fosters had been there to see them off. Freddie still begged to be allowed to go, too, until Henry ordered him to stop being a pest.

Both Simon's mother and father had come to drop him off. Mrs Morgan was a stunningly beautiful woman with long blond hair, starting to grey at the temples. She reminded Wesley of the tiny antelopes called dik-diks that he often saw in the bush. She was bright-eyed and elegant with delicate, dainty legs. Most noticeably, she seemed always alert, ready to flee at the first sniff of danger. She came over to greet Anna while Simon and his father unloaded the car. Wesley had strained to hear their conversation. It was soon apparent that only Mr Morgan was speaking.

"I want to hear that you were first to the top. You are not to be beaten by Neil or one of the others. You are the fittest and you need to get there first." He paused as if expecting an answer, but Simon said nothing and busied himself with the straps of his rucksack. His father went on. "I can't believe you are going to take six days over this walk. I was two years younger than you on my first trip up the mountain, and we did it in three days." Again, Simon made no response. "And don't let that fat boy slow you down. He's going to be a dead weight on this whole journey, mark my words. You don't want to get dragged down by him. He'll slow you all down. He should never have been allowed to come if you ask me." Without warning, Simon spun around to face his father.

DOI: 10.4324/9781003207986-10

"Well, I didn't ask you. Wesley is my friend," growled Simon. "And we're going to do this climb together." He grabbed his rucksack and stalked over to his mother, who hugged him goodbye. She whispered something in his ear and kissed the top of his head. Simon smiled and turned away.

"Well, good luck, Wesley," said Pete, moving uncertainly towards his son.

"It's all right, Dad; you don't need to kiss me," Wesley replied moodily, stung by Mr Morgan's comments.

"Maybe not, but I'm going to hug you!" said Pete, surprising Wesley with a huge bear hug and then pushing him towards the bus. Isla hugged everyone, both her parents, twice, and Pete. She even made Freddie stand still for long enough to be hugged.

"See you on Friday," she called, waving frantically as the school bus pulled away. Anna waved back, blowing kisses to her daughter, abruptly feeling bereft as they drove away. She looked up at Pete, whose eyes were also shiny with tears.

"He'll be fine," she said quietly.

Pete turned to face her. "I know", he replied. "It's just, he's never called me 'Dad' before. No one has ever called me 'Dad'. It takes a bit of getting used to."

"Pete MacKay," she stated. "I do declare that you've let that boy get under your skin. Good for you!" She thumped him playfully on the arm. "Now, toughen up, buttercup. He's off on his first solo adventure."

Despite her confident comments, Anna frowned as she watched the vehicle disappear, experiencing a nagging feeling of apprehension. Isla's waving face was obscured by the billowing dust. Some motherly urge made her want to run after the children and bring them back to the safety of their families. But it was too late. The bus had gone.

Had Anna known the events that would soon unfold on Mount Kenya, she would have never released Isla from her farewell hug. She would have treasured every moment of her daughter's warmth and fizzing enthusiasm. She would not have allowed their laughing children to be driven away, towards peril and calamity. But she did not know.

The dust settled slowly back on to the road in the wake of the departing mini-bus, while the mountain watched and waited in stately, mocking silence.

Wesley allowed the breeze to buffet around him, cooling the sweat on his hot skin. The view below him was magical. Lake Michaelson lay draped across the bottom of the valley, while reflections of the crisp blue sky and scudding clouds glided over its surface. Wesley had never walked above clouds before. They swirled around him like damp ghosts, there one minute and then swept away by a patch of clear sky the next. They poured up the gorge and into the deep glacial valley, driven upwards by the heat of the afternoon sun on the swamps below. The cliffs beneath him were made from a glowing red sandstone, worn by centuries of wind and rain into great pillars and caves. On the far side of the lake, massive grey cliffs rose from the water. It was a mess of scree slopes, crevasses, ledges and dark openings, which surely must contain dragons that emerged on leathery wings to barbecue children at night. The grey cliffs shimmered and sparkled in the sinking sun, where water froze as it emerged from the rocks in brittle, silent, motionless waterfalls. And in this enchanted kingdom they would camp for the night.

It was day three of the climb, and Wesley was having the time of his life. His legs ached, his feet were sore, and he had sunburnt ears, but so did everyone else and they were all in it together. He had not realised just how vast the slopes of Mount Kenya really were. They had not yet seen another human on the walk, despite following a well-trodden trail that was popular with climbers.

He brought his mind back from the view and continued slithering down the steep, sandy path that led to the lake shore. Most of the tracks had been easy underfoot, but this was a steep descent, littered with awkward grass tussocks that were determined to sprain ankles. Between the grass, the soil was soft and slippery as water oozed out of the mountainside in the warmth of the afternoon, only to freeze again to ice after dark. He eventually slid his way to the valley floor, to the welcome smell of stew warming in the pan. He pulled off his rucksack and stretched out on a flat piece of ground, arms and legs apart like a dancing angel. He relished having no weight on his feet and the feel of the sun-warmed earth beneath his back. He closed his eyes and began to hum. Abruptly, he was rudely disturbed by a walking boot pressing on his belly, and he glanced up to see Simon leaning over him, wobbling Wesley's tummy with his right foot.

"Chop chop, you great layabout," Simon laughed. "This tent isn't going to put itself up, you know."

"Slave driver," retaliated Wesley, trying to wallop Simon in the shins, but missing hopelessly. Wesley groaned and heaved himself to his feet. Simon was right: their tent needed to be up before the sun disappeared behind the cliff face. As soon as the sun left the valley, the bitter chill of the night would be upon them.

As he dutifully held tent poles and bashed in the tent pegs, Wesley thought back over the last couple of days. The mountain had been beautiful, very much like the Aberdares, but bigger and even more impressive. The days were crisp and clear until mid-afternoon when clouds started to bubble up over the mountain's flanks, driven by the air rising from the warm earth lower down. The nights were fine, despite being bitterly cold. They had all taken metal water bottles with them, which they filled with hot water before bed, to warm their icy sleeping bags. Wesley had not suffered from the cold as much as the others; he supposed that he was still better covered and so had more insulation than everyone else. He was nicknamed the "human hottie" as he gave off so much heat in the night, and the boys fought over who could sleep next to him for warmth. He had never imagined that there might be a time when being a bit overweight would work to his advantage.

"You'd last much longer than Simon in a famine," commented Neil on the first night. "Simon and Isla would fade away in hours, whereas you'd probably be the last man standing."

"Nah!" retorted Simon "We'd just eat Wesley. That would keep us going for weeks."

"Not if I see you first," countered Wesley, lunging at Simon like a giant slug in his sleeping bag.

"Agghh! I'm being attacked by the human hot-water bottle!" squealed Simon. "Quick, squash it, Neil, before it escapes." Soon the tent was a riot of writhing sleeping bags as the other three boys attempted to flatten Wesley, who was trying to squash them with great squelching noises.

"Go to sleep, you ridiculous boys," a voice thundered from outside the tent.

"Yes, Mr Mwangi," they chorused, wriggling back to their own roll mats.

"Hmm. That warmed me up. I'm not cold anymore," whispered Neil.

"Aha! My cunning plan worked!" hissed Wesley. "I was just warming you up so that I could digest you more easily! Prepare for death by slime!" Wesley oozed off his roll mat flopping on to Neil's legs, which left them all helpless with laughter once again.

What Wesley had not anticipated was that the children talked and chatted and gossiped, and made up stories all day. They talked while they walked. They talked while they put up the tents. They talked around the campfire, and they talked while they fished on the shores of Lake Michaelson. Wesley had found out more about his classmates in three days of walking than he had discovered in nine months at school with them. Neil had confided that he wanted to be an archaeologist, like Indiana Jones.

"Except I'd ditch that silly blonde woman he linked up with in the second film," he decided. "I want to dig up ancient treasures and human bones. Do you know that when an Egyptian pharaoh died, they often buried his servants with him, so that they could serve him in the afterlife?"

"Ugh. I'd hate to be buried alive," commented Isla. "Would you want to dig up people who'd had a horrid death like that?"

Neil considered for a bit. "I think so long as they had been dead for a really, really long time, it would be OK," he said thoughtfully. Then he went on with renewed enthusiasm, "I also want to learn how to dive and explore shipwrecks. Now, they would be OK because most of the bodies would probably have been washed away and eaten by sharks."

And so the conversation turned to shipwrecks and in particular the *Titanic* and how the terrible loss of life might have been avoided in so many ways – if the ship had been going slower . . . if the binoculars had not been left behind so that the lookouts had seen the iceberg earlier . . . if the radio operator in a nearby boat had not been asleep and so had answered her distress calls.

The only thing they did not talk about was Wesley's mother. Wesley did not feel like volunteering information about his past life, and none of the others asked about it. He assumed that Isla had related the grim story of his last few weeks in the UK to the rest of the class, and so felt no need to confide his tragedy again.

On the second night, when the four boys were tucked up in their sleeping bags, Simon had spoken about his father for the first time. It was somehow easier, in the dark, to talk about difficult things.

Wesley had been complaining about Pete's terrible cooking when Simon had joked, "You can't compete when it comes to awful fathers, Wesley. Mine wins hands down."

Wesley was not sure how to respond at first.

Eventually, he said, "Is he as bad at home as he is in public?"

"Yeah. I suppose he is, but at least at home I'm not being shouted at in front of an audience. It always seems worse when everyone else is watching." The boys lay in the dark, waiting to see if Simon would say more. After a while, he continued, "It's as though he has forgotten how to be nice and forgotten that other people have feelings." Simon laughed bitterly. "I'm not sure he's got feelings anymore."

"Was he always like this?" asked Wesley.

"He has been for as long as I can remember, but apparently he used to be fun when he was younger. He was an incredible sportsman, captain of the rugby and hockey teams at school, and he loved tennis, running, cycling – pretty much every sport. He won every competition that he entered and started to play rugby professionally. Mum told me that not long after they were married, there was an accident on the farm. Dad was helping Grandpa build a new barn and some building materials fell on Dad and crushed his legs. It completely smashed his left leg and broke his right thigh and hip. He was unable to walk for nearly a year and had to have lots of operations. It was the year that I was born, so I imagine it was very hard for Mum to look after me and Dad at the same time." Simon paused, staring into the cosy darkness of the tent. "Mum says that he's been lucky. He has learnt to walk again and can drive and fly a helicopter. But he can't really run anymore and hasn't played any sport for twelve years."

"I'm sorry about the accident," said Neil, "but there's no excuse for him to be horrible to you all the time."

"Probably not," sighed Simon. "He's in pain most of the time and that makes him grumpy. He is just always so determined for me to win everything, as if I've got to make up for all the things he can't do now."

"But you do win nearly everything!" exclaimed Wesley.

"Yes, but don't you see – however well I do, it's never good enough."

"Well, I think you're ace," said Wesley quietly.

"Me, too," added Neil and Christopher.

"In fact, this giant human slug thinks you look delicious, just right to be covered in slime and digested." Wesley slurped, squished and oozed in his sleeping bag, lurching over Simon and Neil. Soon the tent was a writhing mass of sleeping bags, again punctuated by squeals of delights and cries of terror.

"Aaahh, it's the revenge of the slug. Grab his legs, Neil, before he gets away."

"Slugs don't have legs," complained Neil. "Quick, he's going to ooze out of the door!"

"Retreat, retreat," was followed by a muffled, "Mmph! I can't – someone's sitting on my head."

"Anyway, how can you retreat when you're trapped in a tent?"

"Go to sleep, you ridiculous boys!" a voice thundered from outside the tent, just as it had the night before.

"Yes, Mr Mwangi," they chorused, oozing back to their own roll mats.

"Hmm, I think Mr Mwangi should be the next victim of the giant slug attack," whispered Wesley.

"I heard that, Wesley," came the stern reply, which just made the tent shake once more with great waves of noisy laughter.

Chapter Ten

When they awoke on the shores of Lake Michaelson, the sun was just cresting the eastern cliff of the valley. It was so cold that the children seemed unable to do anything practical, and they stood around in groups, clutching mugs of tea, watching the light slowly slink towards them as the sun crept higher in the sky. When the sun finally hit them, it was like being thawed by a log fire. Their faces glowed and fingers tingled in the warmth, giving them new energy and joy. Isla wandered down to the edge of the lake, fascinated by the way the surface sparkled and danced. She stood for a long while, taking in the beauty of the spot, and then, out of curiosity, bent down and dipped her fingers into the water. It was bitterly cold, and she noticed a thin layer of ice lying just beneath the surface.

"What would it take to get you to swim in it?" asked a voice from behind her. She turned to see Simon, his eyes alive with mischief. She thought for a while.

"I think . . . only a lifetime guarantee of good health, wealth and happiness would make me swim in that," she answered.

"Done!" he replied, and with no warning, he scooped her up and dangled her over the water. Isla shrieked and tried to wriggle out of his arms.

"You wouldn't dare."

"Wouldn't I?" he puffed, struggling to hold her weight. "I will if you will," he challenged, dropping her back on the lake shore.

 DOI: 10.4324/9781003207986-11

"You won't," she replied.

"I will."

"You're nuts!"

"Probably."

"Darers go first," she challenged.

"Fair enough," he said, starting to undo the laces of his walking boots. "Last one in has to kiss Wesley."

"Yikes," cried Isla, sliding off her trainers, jacket and fleece, while Simon still fought with his laces. The next moment, Isla was down to her vest and leggings. She waded into the water, cracking the thin layer of ice that clung to the edge with her fist. Simon followed her into the water and gasped as his feet and ankles felt as though they were being crushed with cold. With a screech, Isla plunged into the water, gasping as the cold knocked the breath out of her. Not wanting to lose face, Simon was forced to follow. He took a leap into the deeper water and then immediately started paddling for shore, as his whole body threatened to shut down in the cold.

"You have to do three strokes and put your head under or it's not a proper swim," called Isla.

"Are you mad? I'm not putting my head in this," he shouted, as she disappeared under the surface.

She came up squealing, "Jeepers, I think my eyeballs have frozen!" and then laughed and began wading for the shore. "Come on, you great goat, head under or it's a screech, not a swim – it's a Foster family tradition." Simon ducked his head under and did three strokes. He emerged, roaring with pain and fright, and hauled himself out of the water. By this time, the rest of the class was down on the water's edge, utterly astonished at their folly and daring each other to follow suit. Isla and Simon were leaping up and down, partly in a desperate bid to keep warm and partly from the sheer exhilaration of being alive.

"I was definitely first," crowed Isla. "Which means you get to smooch Wesley, lurver-boy."

"Oh, great," sighed Simon. Then he flung his arms open and advanced towards Wesley. "Come and be kissed, Wesley," he shouted. "You're the prize!"

"Kissed? By you?" asked Wesley, looking utterly horrified.

"That's the deal," shouted Simon, breaking into a run. Wesley turned tail and sprinted as fast as he could, which unfortunately wasn't very fast, towards the tents. With the speediest runner in the school hot on his heels, his chances of escape were bleak. Within a few yards, Simon leapt on to his back and planted a kiss on the back of his head, to great whoops of excitement and applause. Wesley turned around and stood with his hands on his hips.

"I'd like you to know," he informed his friends rather huffily, "that when I imagined my 'first kiss', it did not involve another boy attaching his lips to my hair."

"Eugh, Wesley, when did you last wash your hair?" spluttered Simon, wiping his mouth. "I think I just ate some nits."

The children walked steadily for over four hours to reach their highest campsite, located at Simba Col. It felt like a long day. They were all tired from several days of walking, and the air was becoming progressively thinner as they climbed. But despite this, morale was high. Wesley and Isla entertained everyone with terrifying stories of triffids, as they passed more giant lobelias rattling ominously in the breeze.

Wesley felt close to the edge of his endurance as they heaved themselves up the last scrambling climb where they were to pitch their tents. It was as if they had arrived on the moon. The small plateau where they were to camp was completely barren, covered with a scattering of rocks and boulders. Ahead of them was a steep scree slope, up which a thin path climbed, indicating their way to the summit. To their right were the crystal waters of Simba Tarn, a small lake which, despite its beauty, somehow felt chilled and lifeless.

"Thank goodness we don't have to go any further today," sighed Wesley. "What is daunting, though, is the fact that we've been walking for days, and when we get to the top, we have to walk all the way back down."

"Yes, a zip wire down from the summit would be good," responded Neil. "But setting it up would be tricky."

"Hmm," pondered Isla. "All we need is a tea tray."

"What do you mean?" asked Emma.

"Well, at my grandmother's house, we used to nick her tea trays and used them as toboggans to slide down the stairs. It makes your teeth rattle a bit, but you can go really fast. Once I shot straight across the hall and out of the front door."

"Awesome. Imagine how fast we would go down that scree slope on a tray," said Neil, impressed. "They need to update the packing list," he continued in a pompous voice. "One sleeping bag, two pairs of socks, a waterproof and a tea tray."

"One thing is for sure," shivered Isla. "Nothing in the world is going to make me swim in that." She gestured at the icy waters of Simba Tarn. She smiled over at Simon, expecting him to agree, but he was not listening. He was sitting alone, looking away to the east, apparently lost in thought. Wesley wandered over and sat next to him.

"You OK, Si?" he asked. Simon glanced up, startled.

"Yeah. I'm fine," he replied automatically. Wesley frowned.

"Are you sure?" he said. "You look a bit . . . out of it." It seemed to take Simon a while to gather his thoughts enough to respond.

"No, I'm fine, fine. Just tired, that's all."

"Yeah. Me, too," sympathised Wesley. "That was a long climb today," he added, gesticulating at the slope below them, which they had slogged up all afternoon. Simon sank back into uncharacteristic silence. After a while, he put his head in his hands, as if he needed comfort.

"Si, have you got a headache?"

"Yeah. I feel as though my eyeballs are about to explode," he joked.

"Si, you need to talk to Mr Mwangi. You might have altitude sickness. That often starts with a headache, and it can be really dangerous." Simon suddenly smiled brightly.

"Nah. It's just a headache," he said firmly. "I'm fine. Probably just a bit dehydrated. I'll ask Mr Mwangi for some paracetamol." He patted Wesley's shoulder and struggled to his feet. Wesley watched Simon head over to Mr Mwangi's tent. A nagging thought came to the surface of his mind. Mr Morgan had told Simon that he had to be the best, he had to be first to the summit. If Simon got altitude sickness and did not make it to the top, Wesley could imagine the months and years of taunting Simon would get from his father. He realised that Simon was under phenomenal pressure to reach the summit, whereas Pete would be delighted to hear that Wesley had survived this far. *I'll have to keep an eye on him*, thought Wesley, and then he laughed at himself. Simon was the most capable boy here; he certainly didn't need bumbling Wesley (who still struggled to pitch a tent) to keep an eye on him. Mr Mwangi would have it under control. Wesley turned back to gaze at the view. So, he did not see that Simon had failed to find Mr Mwangi in the teachers' tent. Instead of going in search of him, Simon had looked baffled, as if he had forgotten his purpose, and wandered over to the boys' tent to lie down.

Wesley stretched his tired legs on the flat rock at the edge of Simba Col. The sun was behind him, warming his back and casting a glowing, evening light down across the landscape that they had spent the day traversing. He was shattered, but in a satisfying way, with all his limbs tingling with the day's exertion.

"Budge up," said Isla, joining him on the rock and stretching out her legs in the last of the sun. "How are you doing?" she asked.

"Good, and you?"

"Pretty good," she replied. "Although I'm beginning to look forward to a hot bath and a slice of mum's banana cake." Wesley smiled, and they sat in a comfortable silence, staring east. It was Isla who broke the peace.

"You've done really well, Wesley," she said, nudging him with her shoulder. "To be frank, I didn't think you'd make it through the first day, when you announced you were climbing the mountain." Wesley smiled again.

"The day I tried to flatten Simon?" he questioned. Isla nodded. "I had no idea it was a five-day walk! I assumed that people drove most of the way to the top," he laughed. "But once I'd said it, the MacKay stubborn streak got the better of me, and I didn't feel I could back down," he admitted.

"Well, you've coped just as well as the rest of us. You haven't even whinged like you did all the way up the Aberdares."

"Yeah, sorry about that," he said. "It was a bit of a shock. I'd never been hiking before." They stared out at the view, watching the shadows creeping forward each minute, as the sun dropped down below the summit behind them. Eventually, Isla spoke again.

"What was it like being so overweight? I mean, had you always been like that?"

Wesley thought for a bit, trying to put his feelings and ideas into words.

"It was normal," he said eventually. Isla raised her eyebrows in disbelief, so he tried to explain further. "OK. It might not have seemed normal to you, but, to me, being overweight was normal. I have always been overweight, for as long as I can remember, and my mum was overweight. It was just how we were. I don't remember when I went from being overweight to seriously obese – it happened gradually. So, the problems that went with it crept up gradually as well, like not having any friends." He paused, frowning. "The children called me names, but that was how it had always been. I didn't know any different. I was used to not doing much at the weekends and just being with my mum."

"So, what changed?" asked Isla.

"It was when they told me that I had to live with my dad and that he was in the Army. I suddenly looked at myself with new eyes. I imagined what my dad would think of me when he met me for the first time, and that made me feel rubbish. I suddenly became aware of how I must look to others, and yet it felt as though I had no power to change who I was."

"Well, you have changed. The Wesley who arrived in Kenya couldn't walk home, let alone climb the mountain. The determination you've shown has been remarkable." Wesley blushed in the twilight.

"Thanks." He grinned sheepishly at her. "But I couldn't have done it on my own. So many people have helped me. Your mum . . ."

Isla clicked her tongue dismissively. "She's the helping type. She can't stop herself."

Wesley grinned and continued. "Your dad, my dad, all the teachers at school, all the children at school, even that grumpy nurse at the medical centre has been encouraging me every time she weighs me." He laughed, thinking back over the months. "I suppose Simon has helped the most. I was so cross with him for being perfect that I told everyone I would climb Mount Kenya. It was a bit mad, but having a goal to work towards and lots of people supporting me has made it all possible."

"A team effort," murmured Isla.

"Yeah," agreed Wesley. "And being part of a team has been a new experience for me." They lapsed into silence again, looking down over the rocky terrain towards Lake Michaelson. The cold seeped into their bones as the evening sun dropped behind Mount Kenya's summit and they were plunged into shadow. Isla shuddered and turned to head back to the tents.

"Look!" Wesley pointed to the grassland beyond the lake. "Fire." The tell-tale smoke of a bushfire billowed off to one side. Flames glowed and writhed ever brighter in the fading light.

"I hope we get some rain," said Isla. "If that spreads down to the rosewood forest, there will be no stopping it." She looked around her at the barren, rocky landscape. "At least it won't bother us up here. There's nothing to burn."

"Hmm. Strange how something so beautiful can be so destructive," muttered Wesley.

"That's what my dad says about women," said Isla, scrambling to her feet. "Watch out for the beautiful ones. 'They frazzle you up like a bush fire!'"

"But your mum's beautiful, and she's not destructive," defended Wesley, suddenly flushing for having voiced that he thought Anna was beautiful.

"Oh, I'm not so sure," Isla called over her shoulder. "Dad always complains that she's dangerously irresistible!"

No one slept well that night. The cold was so intense that none of them managed to get properly warm, despite having hot-water bottles. Even the boys did not feel like engaging in slug fights. The air was so cold and dry that it sucked the moisture out of their nostrils, causing their noses to hurt. They huddled deep into their sleeping bags, waiting for the hours to pass until they were woken at four a.m. to do the final ascent in the dark. It seemed odd to Wesley to climb to the summit in the dark, but apparently the top often clouded over soon after the sun came up, and so in order to see the view it was best to get there at dawn. He supposed that it would be a shame to walk all this way and not be able to see anything at the top. Despite his nerves, exhaustion soon began to overcome him. He could feel Simon turning restlessly beside him. Wesley wondered if he should check that he was OK, but then abandoned the idea as he drifted off to sleep. Simon was always OK; he was fitter than the rest of them put together.

As Wesley slept, Simon lay shivering in the dark, feeling sick and trying to ignore the steady pounding of his head.

Chapter Eleven

When the children were dug out from their tents at four o'clock in the morning, they were stunned by the cold. Their hands and feet ached, and a fierce breeze whipped around their cheeks and under their hats, despite having them pulled down tightly. The teachers provided them all with hot drinks, which they gulped greedily, cupping them in their gloved hands for warmth.

Simon felt disorientated when he emerged from the tent. Initially, he thought it had snowed in the night until he realised that it was just the moonlight making the volcanic dust and rocks gleam silver in the dark. His brain seemed to be in a fog, and he struggled to tie his laces and gather his warm kit in the darkness. Everything was an effort, as if he was walking through treacle. His mental focus was not helped by the dull, thudding headache that made him feel as though his eyes were bulging in their sockets. Before he'd had time for a drink, Mr Mwangi was calling everyone to line up. The others were chatting excitedly, but Simon didn't seem able to form any words. All the children were virtually unrecognisable with scarves pulled up to their noses and hats covering their eyebrows. He lined up behind Neil. Wesley, who was always useless at getting ready quickly, was behind him. One guide and Mrs Wambui were at the front, and Mr Mwangi and the second guide brought up the rear. The nervous group moved off slowly up the scree slope, finding their way by the light of their head torches.

Wesley had never experienced such bitter cold. He thought that he would warm up when they got moving, but

   DOI: 10.4324/9781003207986-12

they walked slowly due to the lack of oxygen in the air, and so warm blood never seemed to make it to his toes. He tried to chat to Simon a couple of times, but the other boy seemed lost in thought, concentrating on navigating the route in the darkness. Wesley noted that the light from his torch seemed to be fading and he cursed himself for forgetting to change the batteries the night before.

Simon was struggling to focus against the relentless pounding of his head and so had not quite kept pace with the others, leaving a gap between him and Neil in front. At one point, the track wound in an S-shape between large boulders, which meant that for a short time Simon lost sight of Neil's torch ahead. It was at this point that Mr Mwangi's shoelace came undone and he stopped, fumbling to tie it with cold, tired fingers.

Wesley, who was close behind Simon, was surprised to see him suddenly veer off to the left. Wesley had been sure he had seen Neil head round to the right, so he called out to his friend.

"Hey, Simon, that's the wrong way." Simon did not seem to hear, so Wesley stumbled after him and eventually caught him by the arm. "Simon, you've gone the wrong way," he confirmed.

"This way. Got to get there first. It all makes sense," muttered Simon irritably.

"What?!" replied Wesley, not understanding what Simon was rambling about, but Simon had moved off again along the top of a scree slope where there did not seem to be a path at all. Wesley caught him by the arm again. "Simon, we've got to go back," he cautioned. Simon tried to shake him off crossly.

"It's this way," he hissed and stepped out into a black void.

Wesley still had hold of Simon when he fell and so was dragged forward by the other boy's weight. He instinctively tried to balance himself and gripped Simon's arm fiercely to halt his friend's fall, but his feet began to slide on the loose scree, and he found that he was slipping uncontrollably down the mountainside. He tried to call out but dropped heavily off a small cliff, and the landing knocked the air out of his lungs. After that, he tumbled, crashing against rocks, sliding in an avalanche of small stones and gravel. Simon's arm was soon wrenched from his grasp, and he skidded down and down, alone in the darkness into the black abyss below.

Meanwhile, Mr Mwangi finished tying his lace and accepted the offer of chocolate from the guide who was waiting behind him. They rounded the corner and were surprised to see that the trail of torch lights was a little further ahead than they had expected. They lengthened their stride and fell in behind Neil, the last of the children in the line. In the darkness, they were unaware that two of their charges had fallen into the abyss below.

Wesley's fall took less than a minute, but it felt as though he had fallen through the centre of the earth. He came to rest in a crumpled heap, too stunned to notice the bruises, scrapes and cuts he had sustained on the way down. His first thought was that he was struggling to breathe, partly due to being winded and partly from the panic of having fallen off a mountain in the darkness. He willed himself to breathe, taking in great gulps of freezing air. He was too terrified to move, in case he was perched on a ledge and any movement might send him plummeting further down into the dark. He felt utterly disorientated and alone, until he remembered Simon.

"Simon!" he called out, but his mouth was so full of dirt that the sound emerged as a pathetic croak. "Simon!" he called again into the darkness. He felt for his head torch but only found a sore patch on his forehead where the torch had been. His eyes were so full of debris that he was not sure if it was pitch-black or he was just blinded by dirt. The wind whipped across his face, stinging the raw skin. He instinctively reached for the hood of his jacket to protect himself from the wind, and in pulling it up felt a hard lump lodged in the hood. By some miracle, his head torch had been caught in his hood as he fell. He pulled it out and his immediate surroundings were lit up with a faint yellow beam. He had fallen to the bottom of a very steep scree slope, which flattened out into a rocky area. To his left was a black mass, which he realised was a small lake caught in the hollow at the bottom of the slope. On the edge of the lake, partly in the water, was a red heap, which lay listless, like a bag of rubbish discarded from the mountain path above. With the shock of the fall and the numbing cold, Wesley's brain was working slowly. He just stared at the red blob, so out of place against the natural colours of the mountainside. Until the thought came to him: Simon was wearing a red jacket.

With sudden energy, Wesley tried to scramble to his feet but kept slipping on the rough, gravelly terrain.

"Simon! Simon! I'm coming," he rasped as he lurched towards the lifeless figure. As he approached, the desperateness of the situation became apparent. Simon was lying face down in the water with his legs awkwardly jammed up against a rock. He was completely still. Wesley grasped his torso, dragging it out of the shallow water and on to the jagged shoreline. His fingers felt immediately chilled by freezing black water that had soaked Simon to the waist. Simon's face was ghost-white in the places where it was not horribly battered. His lips were blue, and it was clear he was not breathing.

"Simon!" shouted Wesley, feeling panic envelop him again. "Breathe, Simon! Breathe!" The body made no response. Thoughts raced wildly through Wesley's mind. *I need help. I need a doctor. I need my dad. Someone will help. Mr Mwangi will help. It will be too late. He's not breathing. What do I do? I'm too pathetic to help.* But Wesley was determined. He had spent years watching medical dramas on TV with his mother and he'd seen what the medics did when people drowned. He had not been able to help his mother when she drowned in the freezing waters of the river Swale, so he was determined not to fail now, when he had a chance to save his friend. With clumsy fingers, he unzipped Simon's jacket, tilted his head back and pinched his nose, Wesley blew two lungfuls of air into the lifeless body. He followed up the breaths with five hard presses on Simon's breast bone and then more breaths. He was not sure he was doing it right. He felt the situation was probably hopeless, but he was determined to try and prayed to all the gods in the heavens to allow Simon to live. He was leaning down to give a fourth set of breaths when Simon's body suddenly heaved and spluttered and coughed, and finally began breathing independently.

Wesley hollered at the rocks and water and mountain air. "You're alive! You're alive! Simon, you're going to be OK!" he shouted. Simon made no reply, but lay panting and coughing with his eyes closed.

Wesley realised that Simon might not be conscious and turned the other boy's face towards him in concern.

Simon grimaced. "Christ, get off, Wesley! You weigh a tonne," he complained. Wesley burst into tears of relief and gathered Simon into his arms and sobbed. He cried for about half a minute before a muffled voice from his shoulder mumbled. "Wesley, you're still really, really heavy. Get off, you great oaf!" Wesley smiled and tried to gather his wits.

"Simon, thank goodness you're OK. I thought you'd drowned," he spluttered through the tears. He looked around and realised that it was not just him who was squashing Simon, but that his legs were wedged under a rock. Although it was uncomfortable, the rock may have prevented him from tumbling into the deeper waters of the lake. Carefully, he wriggled Simon's legs free one by one, and then began to assess the damage as his friend gingerly sat up.

Simon's right arm was obviously broken and hanging cumbersomely by his side. A deep gash oozed above his right eye, and his face was terribly scraped and bashed. What was most immediately apparent was that he was chilled to the bone. His clothes were drenched in icy water from the lake, and Wesley knew that if he did not do something fast, Simon was going to die of hypothermia.

"My arm," Simon shivered. "It hurts."

"I'm afraid it's broken. I'll strap it up to keep it still. But, Simon, we need to get you a bit warmer."

"Arm," muttered Simon again. Very carefully, Wesley peeled off Simon's jacket and lifted his fleece over his head. It was so painful to get the broken arm out of the fleece that Wesley used his penknife to cut and rip off Simon's thermal top.

"I liked that top," muttered Simon with a wry smile, before closing his eyes again, wincing in pain.

The boys made a sling from Wesley's scarf and tied Simon's arm securely across his chest. Wesley wrenched off his rucksack and dug out the spare fleece he had been carrying. He then pulled the dry fleece over Simon's head, took off his own jacket, which was mainly dry, and carefully negotiated it over Simon's good arm.

This was all hard to achieve by the fading light of his torch. He shook the torch fiercely, but all it produced was a tiny, dull puddle of light. He knew that he needed to get Simon off the mountain fast, but in the pitch darkness, he could not see enough to establish if there was a way out from the lake. He would have to wait until dawn. He searched around for a sheltered space between two boulders and sat against the cold rocks hugging Simon in front of him, willing him to stay warm. Simon had an emergency blanket in the bottom of his rucksack and Wesley wrapped it around the two of them the best he could.

"It won't be long now, Simon," he said encouragingly. "As soon as the light comes up, we'll find a way out of here." His voice suggested optimism, but, inside, Wesley's mind was whirling from panic to despair.

"Talk to me," Simon said. "Talk to me. Keep me awake." Wesley knew that Simon was right. He needed something to pass the time and help him to focus so that he didn't let go. But for once Wesley's brain was empty of anything useful to say. He wasn't like Isla's dad who always knew how to cheer people up, even when they were hanging upside down by their seatbelts in a ditch.

"I don't know what to say," he murmured apologetically. He knew he must make an effort, but his mind seemed numbed by the shock, the altitude and the cold.

"Tell me about your mum," replied Simon.

"My mum?" Wesley repeated.

"Yes, you've never talked about her. You've never told us what happened."

"I thought you knew. I thought Isla would have told you."

"Nope," replied Simon, suddenly gasping with pain as he shifted his position slightly. "She said that it wasn't her story to tell."

"Huh," smiled Wesley. "She said the same thing to me when I wanted to know about your dad."

"Girls," muttered Simon. "Go on, talk." So Wesley began to paint a picture of how his previous life had been, so different from their current situation that he would have never believed was possible a year ago.

"Mum was lovely. She had thick, dark hair and kind eyes. Yes, kind. That's the best way to describe her. She used to be kind. We didn't go out much; she was always short of money and didn't seem to want to spend time with other people. I don't know if she had any friends. I think she'd had a job in a shop but gave it up when I was born. Mum used to see her parents most days, but first her mother and then her father died, not long after I was born. So, it was just the two of us. Some days she'd be fun and we'd have pancakes for breakfast and she'd chat all the way to school. But on other days she didn't get up at all. She once said that, on the bad days, it was as if the duvet was too heavy for her to get out of bed. The doctor said she was depressed and gave her some tablets, but I'm not sure they helped much." Wesley smiled to himself. "She liked to eat. We both liked to eat. It seemed to make everything feel better. Saturday nights were always good. We'd go to the supermarket together and buy crisps, pizza and chips and a huge packet of chocolate mini-rolls. Then we'd go home and watch TV. She liked medical dramas best and talent shows. There was always something good on telly on a Saturday night." He stopped, unable to go on. The happy memory was snatched away to be replaced by the bitter reality that his mother was dead.

"Go on," murmured Simon.

Wesley sniffed and shifted his position beneath Simon's weight. His mind wandered back to that day when he had come home from school to find the flat empty. He explained how he had waited as the evening darkened into night, imagining what his mum would say when she opened the door . . . *Sorry I'm late, love, I just had to nip down to the shops.* When darkness fell and it became too late for the shop scenario to be plausible, he imagined more unusual situations such as . . . *Sorry I'm late, love, but I saw a woman knocked down in the road and had to wait to give a statement to the police . . .* or *Sorry I'm late, I tripped and broke my leg, but my phone battery ran out so I couldn't call from the hospital.* But she did not come home that night. She did not give an explanation.

Wesley had woken the following morning and could not think what to do. He did not know any of the neighbours, and calling the police seemed overly melodramatic, as if admitting to himself that something was seriously wrong. So, he put on his uniform, had some cereal and went to school.

He was sure she would be home when he came back that evening, with a story to tell. Perhaps she had had an adventure. But as he unlocked the door of the flat, he could sense a hollowness in his surroundings, a dull emptiness and the certain knowledge that he was totally alone.

He fell into a new routine, gradually eating everything that was left in the flat. Rushing home after school to see if she was there and then waiting throughout the evening, unable to leave, in case she came home expecting to find him. It wasn't until the fourth day that the food ran out and he shuffled to school with an empty stomach. His teacher, Mrs Rogers, called him over at the end of the lesson before break. She had asked him if he was OK, because he seemed out of sorts, and that was when he had started to sob.

Everything had happened frighteningly fast after that. He was given tea and toast in the staff room, and then the police had arrived. He had to answer endless questions about his mother, when he had last seen her, what she looked like and what clothes she was wearing. Then the woman with the soft voice and sad eyes had told him about the body that had been found in the River Swale on Monday night. It was a very large woman with dark hair and a blue opal ring on her right hand. He knew it was his mum, even before they mentioned the ring. Wesley confirmed that his mum couldn't swim, so it was not surprising that she did not survive the racing, peaty waters of the River Swale. Various people talked about it being a shocking accident, so tragic, such a waste. But he could see in their eyes the question that no one dared to voice: Was it an accident, or did she mean to kill herself?

He was sent to live with Mrs Hawthorn, a foster carer, who lived near Northallerton. He had to start at a new school nearby. It was obvious that the children had been told to be sympathetic to the new boy. He heard them whispering in the playground.

"Who's the fat boy?"

"He's the one whose mother died."

For as long as he could remember, Wesley had been known as the "fat boy". It was the way in which he was so obviously different from everyone else that no one ever bothered to describe his height, hair, eyes or personality. Now he simply became "the fat boy with the dead mum".

He would never forget Mrs Hawthorn's smiling face when she told him the "wonderful news" that the police had tracked down his father. Within a short time, he had flown to Kenya to live with a man he had never met before.

"You know the rest," he said and paused, waiting for a response. "Simon?"

"Yes. I know the rest," Simon replied groggily. Wesley sighed.

"I find it hard to think about her now. I know she loved me, but I feel furious with her for not having loved me enough to live for me. Then I feel guilty for enjoying my life here. My life is better without her. How can I say that about my own mother?"

"Funny things, mothers," mumbled Simon.

"Yeah! Look at the grief Isla's mum has given me this year."

"You fancy her," stated Simon.

"No, I don't!" exploded Wesley. "She's old."

"You still fancy her," teased Simon.

"Don't," persisted Wesley, digging Simon in the ribs, which made him groan. "Oops, sorry. Well, you fancy Isla."

"So do you," shot back Simon, not even bothering to deny his own feelings.

"No, I don't. She'll probably grow up to be dangerously irresistible," said Wesley knowingly. "Oh, all right. Of course we both fancy her. There, satisfied?"

"Ha! Knew it," replied Simon, flinching again. "God, Wesley. Everything hurts. I think my brain is about to explode."

"Yuk, no exploding heads, please. Think of the mess."

Wesley glanced desperately around, and it was a great relief to realise that a pale grey light now surrounded them, enabling him to make out the landscape more clearly. He looked up at the mountainside above them. He saw they had fallen over a small cliff and then down a massive scree slope. The path to the summit was now a couple of hundred metres above them and there was no hope of climbing back up. However, it might be possible to skirt around the edge of the lake and over the ridge at the end. The sun was dimly rising from that direction, which suggested it would be roughly the right way to head back to the campsite. They were completely hidden from the summit path, and Wesley realised that it was likely that Mr Mwangi had not seen their fall in the darkness.

"I've got to be first," muttered Simon.

"What? It's a bit late for that. Simon, we've got to get back to the campsite. Your arm needs to be put in plaster," replied Wesley calmly, while trying not to think too much about the blood seeping from Simon's forehead, where a large bruise was rapidly swelling under a deep gash.

"The tallest one is the third from the right," replied Simon.

"What?" retorted Wesley again, but Simon did not reply; he seemed to be dozing off. Wesley pushed Simon up, reached under his good arm and hauled him to his feet.

"Simon, you've got to walk. We need to get help from the campsite. Help me, Simon. You've got to walk."

"OK. Let's walk. It's not far to the top now," murmured Simon.

The ungainly pair slowly stumbled along the lake shore as if they were in a drunken three-legged race. Simon initially seemed unable to balance on his legs, but as they progressed, they became accustomed to their new shuffling gait. Wesley was aching from head to toe and felt as though he'd been put in a tumble drier with a load of boulders. Every joint shouted with pain as he began to walk, swaying with Simon's additional weight. Each glance at Simon reminded him that his friend's life was in his hands. At times, Simon talked sense, but he often repeated himself and sometimes said things that were completely incomprehensible. Wesley understood enough about altitude sickness and head injuries to know that he had to get Simon off the mountain as quickly as possible.

The rest of the school party were unaware of the crisis as they trudged their way to the summit. The cold was so bitter that they were all cocooned in their own private thoughts. As everyone was so wrapped up against the cold, it was hard to tell who was who, and so it was easy not to realise that two of their number were missing. Mr Mwangi heaved himself up the metal rungs that led to the peak and was stunned by the sparkling vista that was laid before him. He felt on top of the world, with Kenya stretching away into the distance. He could see all the way to Mount Kilimanjaro to the South and Mount Elgon to the North. Everyone was chattering and cheering, delighted to have made it to the top with no problems. He clapped the figure who had been in front of him on the back, thinking it was Wesley, and was surprised when Neil turned his smiling face towards him.

"Congratulations Neil," Mr Mwangi said, slightly puzzled. "A great climb." Then, looking past Neil, he said, "But where's Wesley?"

"He and Simon were behind me," Neil replied. "I thought they were just in front of you."

A terrible sense of foreboding flooded through Mr Mwangi and Neil as they desperately looked around their fellow climbers. Mr Mwangi swiftly took charge, emitting a loud whistle, which brought everyone to a standstill.

"Simon! Wesley!" he called. "Where are Simon and Wesley?"

Now that the sun had risen, it was immediately apparent that the boys were nowhere to be seen, and after some quick questioning, Mr Mwangi realised that no one had spoken to them since they had left the campsite. How could he have been so stupid? Why had he not chatted to the boy in front of him? Mr Mwangi blamed himself. He realised that it was because the boy in front had been chatting happily with the person ahead of him and he had thought it was Wesley talking to Simon. Only now did he realise that he had been watching Neil talking to Isla.

Most of the class were now in tears, desperately worried about their classmates, on top of being cold and exhausted themselves.

While Mrs Wambui comforted them, Mr Mwangi fished out his phone and fervently prayed for a signal so he could call for help.

Chapter Twelve

In the frozen dawn gloom, Wesley and Simon reached the end of the lake and began to scramble up the pile of glacial moraine that blocked the end of the gulley. Wesley had no idea what to expect on the far side of the slope and desperately hoped it would not be a cliff, or that the terrain would force them to head south, further away from the summit path. The further they strayed from the path, the less likely it was that they would be found if they could not make their way back to the campsite. He knew that if they got lost, they might never be found. As they crawled their way to the top of the slope, he was relieved to see that there was a short drop on the other side and then a possible route through some huge boulders up to the left, towards where he thought the path might be.

Simon lay at the top of the slope, groaning with each breath. He seemed to be asleep. *I must keep him awake*, thought Wesley, but he felt drained of all energy now that the adrenaline of the fall had worn off. He lay with his arm around Simon, aching with cold, trying to muster the strength to continue. On cue, the morning sun peeped above the cliff to the east and its warming rays fell upon them. The heat was so intense that it was like walking into a hot shower after a cold swim. Wesley pulled off his hood and allowed the sun to warm his face, filling his tired body with energy and courage, like a mother's hug. He breathed deeply, enjoying the warmth.

"Great!" he observed at last "We've just nearly frozen to death and now I'll probably get sunburnt. Simon, I need

DOI: 10.4324/9781003207986-13

you to walk," he said with authority. "I'm taking you home. Come on, Simon, you have to help me! We're going to do this together."

"OK. OK. I'm coming," muttered Simon, hauling himself to his feet with Wesley's help. Together, they slithered, stumbled and crawled through the boulders and up the next slope and two more after that.

When they came to the third crest, Wesley's heart leapt as he saw below him the brightly coloured tents of their campsite nestled beside Simba Tarn, which was now a radiant blue-green in the early-morning sunshine. At the camp, he could see a handful of porters making breakfast and starting to dismantle the tents.

"Look, Simon! Look! We've made it. There's the camp. We're nearly there."

Simon painfully sucked in his breath. "Well done, Wes."

"How about some tea and biscuits?" replied Wesley cheerfully.

"Feeling a bit sick," Simon replied, sagging against Wesley again. They slid down the scree slope towards the camp, slowly so as not to trip and fall again.

"Where is a tea tray when you need one?" gasped Wesley. "We could slide down this in a second if we only had a decent tea tray."

"Mr Mwangi will probably have one in his pocket," responded Simon weakly. "He always seems prepared for anything."

As they came a little closer, Wesley began to shout and wave his free arm. To begin with, this had no effect, then suddenly one of the figures below looked up and a moment later three men began to run, scrambling up the rocks towards them. Wesley sank to his knees as two of the porters took Simon's weight from him. The third man helped him up and guided him to the camp. He found he was shaking as he accepted sweet tea.

The men were trying to stem the bleeding from Simon's head, but it was clear that he needed urgent medical help, which they could not provide here on the mountain. Desperately, he asked the porters for a phone and dialled the only number he knew by heart. He called his father.

"Dad! It's me, Wesley."

"Hi, Wes! Great to hear from you," replied Pete. "I can only just hear you. You're breaking up a bit. How's it going?" Pete waited for a reply, but all he could hear was sobbing down the phone. "Wesley, what's happened? Tell me. I'll try to help." Wesley desperately tried to control his breathing, but the relief of speaking to his dad, someone who could take the hideous responsibility of saving Simon away from him, was too much. He began to sob once more. Pete allowed the boy to cry for a short while and then cut in again.

"Wesley, something has obviously gone wrong. Tell me what has happened. If you are injured, we may need to get help fast." Wesley took great shuddering breaths and then blurted out the main details of the story.

"I think Simon's got altitude sickness. He was confused on the walk up and we fell in the darkness. I don't think anyone saw us fall because no one came to help. Simon landed face down in a lake. He wasn't breathing, Dad! I thought he was dead. I had to get him breathing again." Wesley began crying once more. Pete's knuckles went white as he gripped the phone. The image of Wesley alone on Mount Kenya trying to save Simon's life made him cold with fear. Wesley blundered on with his account.

"Dad, I managed to find my way back to the campsite, but only the porters are here and they don't speak much English. Simon's really bad, Dad. His arm is broken, and his head is bleeding. He keeps repeating himself and falling asleep."

Although Pete was sitting in his underpants in his bedroom far below in Nanyuki, he took charge of the situation on the mountain straight away.

"Wesley, you've been amazing. You have done all the right things. I'm going to get a helicopter to bring Simon down." Wesley felt a flood of relief. All he had to do was wait and the helicopter would rescue them, he thought, until his father continued. "Wesley, I'm going to need you to get Simon down to Shipton's Hut. It is too high for the helicopter to land at Simba Tarn, and if Simon has got altitude sickness, the faster we can get him lower down, the better."

Wesley burst into tears again. He couldn't bear the thought of dragging Simon further down the mountain. He didn't want to be in charge anymore. He was exhausted, shaking and increasingly aware of his own bruises and scrapes. It hurt when he breathed and there was something wrong with his left wrist.

Pete continued his instructions with a firm ring of authority in his voice, "Wesley, take two porters with you to help carry Simon and guide the way. Try to keep Simon warm. Talk to him. I will have help waiting at Shipton's. Keep this phone with you, so I can keep in touch."

"I don't know if I can do it, Dad," sniffed Wesley.

"Of course you can!" replied his father with confidence. "You're my son. I know you can do it."

Wesley put the phone in his pocket and explained the situation to the porters, speaking in English and the little Kiswahili that he knew. They were highly practical men, who were strong and fit and knew the mountain well. Within a few minutes, a makeshift stretcher for Simon had been made, and with a man at each end, the small party headed off past Simba Tarn and up the short incline on the other side. When they scrambled to the top, Wesley was aghast at what he saw. Ahead of them, a massive scree slope fell away below them, dropping precipitously several hundred feet. There was no sign of Shipton's Hut or any other form of civilisation on the great expanse of mountain that spread before them. Wesley stopped, overwhelmed again by the hopelessness of the situation, but the porters had not paused at the top. They set off on a sure-footed slipping, sliding walk down the scree with the stretcher swaying between them. Wesley tottered after them, terrified at first as the scree beneath his feet began to slide. After a while, he became accustomed to allowing himself to slither with the tumbling stones. In this way, they almost ran down the mountainside in huge sliding steps, hoping that they did not trip and tumble to the bottom. Eventually, they reached the foot of the slope and began to traverse a gentle path along a deep glacial valley. The land was no longer barren but covered in lush grass and moss, and, increasingly, the familiar giant lobelias lined their way.

Simon groaned with the movement of the stretcher, his good arm lolling limply over the side. Wesley took his hand and squeezed. It felt cold and there was no squeeze in return.

"Simon?" Wesley called. "Can you hear me?" Simon dimly opened his eyes but made no response. *Talk to him*; that was what his father had said. So Wesley began to chatter.

"You're going to be OK, Simon. It's not far now. A helicopter and a medic are going to meet us at Shipton's, and they'll get you sorted out. You are going to be OK. I command it!" he said jokingly. The hand gave him a faint squeeze in return, which made Wesley gulp back fresh tears. The lobelias reminded him of the story that Isla's dad had told them about triffids when he had climbed the Aberdares with the Fosters. So he blundered on.

"I'm going to tell you the story of the triffids. You need to listen to it so that you can remember it and tell your children when you climb the mountain with them in years to come. Although you're going to have to start washing more if you want to get married and have children," he teased. "First you kiss my hair and then make me do mouth-to-mouth resuscitation on you in a lake. I can tell you now that I'm not doing that again unless you start cleaning your teeth more often. Eww!"

"You can't talk," murmured Simon. "Your hair was revolting." Wesley smiled.

"Anyway, the story goes that there was a scientist who worked on a triffid farm. Triffids are extraordinary plants that are found in the jungles of Africa. I forget why they were farming them in the UK – something to do with a useful oil they produced, I think. Anyway, triffids can move around on weird root-like legs. So imagine if you planted one at the end of your garden, you might wake up in the morning and find it had slurped its way up the garden in the night and was snuggled up against the kitchen window. The other thing is that they were not very cuddly. They were meat eaters and used to kill their prey by lashing out with a sting that blinded people, and then the triffid would slowly digest you. Because they had a habit of slinking off and eating people, the triffids had to be kept in farms surrounded by huge electric fences." Wesley rambled on, stumbling beside the stretcher and clutching Simon's hand, as the porters hurried down the length of the valley.

By the time Shipton's Hut came into view in the distance, Simon was not responding anymore, but Wesley continued talking, encouraging, willing him not to let go. When they still had about a kilometre to go, one of the porters heard the distant patter-patter of helicopter blades and gestured to a dark blemish, which rose over the horizon and headed steadily up the valley. Wesley could see the pilot as the aircraft gently circled above them. He gave them a thumbs-up and headed back to land near the mountain hut. Wesley's eyes filled with tears once more, and it was a while before he could speak again to Simon.

"They're here, Simon. The doctor is here. You're going to be OK," he said, but the figure on the stretcher lay cold and still.

As they neared the hut, a group of men rushed towards them and took the stretcher from the exhausted porters. Wesley refused to let go of Simon's hand and struggled to keep up on wobbly legs as they powered towards the helicopter, which now sat with drooping blades like a tired bird.

"Simon? My name is Dr Juma. I'm going to help you," said an open-faced man who came alongside the stretcher. "You must be Wesley," he said, looking over Simon to the other ashen boy. The doctor put his arm on Wesley's shoulder. "Well done," he said quietly. "Now, tell me what you know."

"His arm is broken. I tied it up the best I could with a scarf. He was confused before he fell and then bashed his head on the way down. He was face down in a lake when I found him and not breathing. I had to do mouth-to-mouth." The doctor raised his eyebrows, obviously impressed, and indicated for Wesley to continue. "He said it hurt when he breathed, and he's been repeating himself and falling asleep a lot."

"OK. Thank you, Wesley. That is really helpful. Let's sort him out, shall we? Can you help by coming on the helicopter with us down to Nairobi? I'm sure Simon would be comforted to know that you were there." Wesley nodded mutely, tears streaming down his battered face.

Chapter Thirteen

Pete had been busy in the hours since Wesley's phone call. First, he had tasked a helicopter to collect the boys. Then he had contacted Mrs Omwoto, the headteacher, who had cried with relief when she heard that the boys had been found. His phone call had come only a few minutes after Mr Mwangi's desperate call from the summit, explaining that Simon and Wesley were missing somewhere near the peak.

By chance, Simon's parents were in Nairobi and so were already waiting at the hospital for the helicopter to arrive. Pete had started driving south as soon as he could and was now battling through the Nairobi traffic towards the hospital.

The flight passed in a blur for Wesley, who spent the journey gripping Simon's hand. He slowly became aware that the steep, densely cultivated valleys had given way to houses and roads, shadowed by giant jacaranda trees laden with blue flowers. He could hear the pilot clearing the area for landing as they circled the sports pitch by the hospital. An ambulance was parked in the corner and various people waited to receive them. As soon as they landed, Simon's body was swept away, surrounded by the

 DOI: 10.4324/9781003207986-14

emergency medical team. Wesley found it hard to climb out of the helicopter with stiff, bruised limbs. A nurse came over to guide him towards a waiting stretcher. He saw Simon's mother bending over her son, talking to him, kissing his forehead. Then he saw Simon's father gazing at him with undisguised hatred. Before Wesley had steadied himself on the ground, Mr Morgan marched over and jabbed him in the chest, almost knocking him off his feet.

"I should have known!" he bellowed. "I should have known that this would be your fault. You are a liability. You should have never been allowed on that trip. You pathetic waster!"

The horrified nurse pushed herself between Wesley and Mr Morgan.

"That is no way to speak to a child," she retorted firmly.

"This loser has nearly killed my son!" Simon's father roared, at which something inside Wesley snapped. All the terror, stress and pain of the morning turned to anger at this man, this bully, who made Simon's life a misery. Wesley stepped round the nurse and looked boldly up at Mr Morgan.

"If anyone is responsible for this accident, it's you!" he spat. "You put so much pressure on Simon that he didn't tell anyone when he had altitude sickness. Simon fell because he was confused, because he was too scared to stop, because you would bully him about not getting to the top first. Don't you dare blame this on me! If it wasn't for me, Simon would be dead, face down in a lake on the top of the mountain." With a surprising show of strength, Wesley pushed Mr Morgan in the chest making him stagger back and then lurched past the man towards the waiting stretcher.

The nurse followed Wesley, giving Mr Morgan a prim little prod in the chest for good measure as she passed.

It was not until the following day that Wesley saw Simon again. Wesley had been desperate to visit but was scared of bumping into Mr Morgan after their argument. Pete waited until they saw Mr Morgan leave and then helped Wesley along the corridor to Simon's room. Mrs Morgan stood up as Wesley knocked and shyly peered around the door.

"Ah, Wesley, come in, come in. I came to see you last night, but you were asleep," she said warmly. She crossed the room and enveloped him in a motherly hug, giving him a huge kiss on the top of his head. "I can never thank you enough," she said, planting another kiss on his hair.

"I wouldn't do that, Mum," murmured a voice from the bed. "I think he's got nits."

"I don't care," replied Mrs Morgan. "I'm happy to kiss him, nits and all," placing a third kiss on Wesley's head.

"Why is your family always kissing me?" complained Wesley, with a huge grin and rather pink cheeks.

"Perhaps it has something to do with saving my life?" suggested Simon. Wesley went over to him. Simon's arm was in plaster and he had a neat line of stitches above his eyebrow. His face was a mess of scrapes and bruises, just like Wesley's.

"How are you doing?" asked Wesley.

"They operated on my arm this morning. It should be fine in a couple of months. I've got concussion, but I'm feeling a bit better today. Just please don't make me laugh. I've got broken ribs and it hurts like hell when I laugh."

"Me, too," agreed Wesley. "It feels fine so long as I don't breathe or eat or move."

"Hmm, great. This is going to be a fun few weeks," said Simon grimly. "What's up with your arm?" Wesley held up the plaster on his left wrist.

"Fractured radius, but not serious," he replied. Wesley paused, looking down on his friend. "Simon, how much do you remember?"

"Bits and pieces," Simon replied thoughtfully. "I remember you trying to stop me going off the path. I don't remember the fall or landing in the lake or you giving me the kiss of life."

"I'm glad. You weren't looking your best," joked Wesley.

"I remember being cold – aching with cold – and you giving me your dry clothes. You told me about your mum. I remember being tired and everything hurting and triffids. I remember you talking about triffids." He smiled. "Was I a bad patient?" he asked.

"Terrible," laughed Wesley. "If you do it again. I might leave you in the lake next time."

Simon was suddenly serious. "Wesley, I know you saved my life yesterday and I know that we both could have died falling down that slope, all because I didn't tell Mr Mwangi I was suffering from the altitude. It was stupid of me. It was all my fault and I'm sorry I dragged you into it."

"Simon, it was an accident. You weren't thinking straight. No one meant it to happen."

"I know," Simon said, swallowing hard. "But whatever the cause, I need to say thank you. You saved my life and I'll never forget it. So, thank you."

"You're welcome," replied Wesley simply.

"And thank you from me, too," cried Mrs Morgan, wrapping him in a bear hug from behind and kissing his hair for a fourth time. Wesley went pink again and secretly felt glad he had washed his hair the night before. Mrs Morgan turned Wesley to face her.

"Wesley, I need to apologise for what my husband said to you yesterday. It was unforgivable for him to blame you for the accident. He knows now how much we are in your debt. He is a proud man and may need a bit of time to come to terms with everything. Do you mind waiting until he is ready to say sorry in his own way?"

"Of course not," said Wesley graciously, keen to avoid a meeting with Mr Morgan if at all possible. Pete joined the conversation.

"We partly came to say goodbye. The doctor is discharging Wesley this afternoon, so I plan to take him back to Nanyuki this evening."

"We hope that Simon will be home tomorrow as well," said Mrs Morgan. "They just want to keep him here for one more night for observation."

"That's great," replied Pete, "I'm so glad that you are recovering well, Simon. But you look as though you need some sleep, so I'm going to drag Wesley away. We'll come and see you at home when you feel up to it."

"Thanks, Sergeant MacKay," Simon said.

Pete took Wesley's good arm and led him to the door.

Chapter Fourteen

A week later, Wesley was lining up for the end-of-term assembly. He was nervously holding his script, as all the Year 6 pupils were doing speeches on how they felt about leaving the school. Wesley had not known what to write. He had such mixed emotions as this had been the very worst and the very best year of his life. In the past twelve months, he had lost his mother and his home. He had met his father, attended three schools, met the Fosters and fallen a little bit in love with Isla (and if he was really honest with himself, he felt rather fluffy about Anna and Simon's mother as well – but in a motherly sort of way, of course). He had lost weight, climbed to the top of the Aberdares, been trapped upside down in a Land Rover and learnt to swim in rivers. He had failed to climb to the top of Mount Kenya and had saved his friend's life. It had been a struggle to summarise such a massive whirl of emotions into the few lines that he clutched in his hand for the assembly.

Wesley had returned to school the day after the rest of his class, who had successfully conquered Mount Kenya. He was greeted as the long-lost hero that he was. He was repeatedly hugged by teachers and children of all ages. Many of the little children didn't know what he had done, but hugged him anyway, because it seemed to be the thing to do. Everyone wanted to hear his story, to sign his plaster cast and generally spend time with such a brave and noteworthy member of the school. For the first time in his life, Wesley found he was popular. Even better, he was popular for behaving in a way that made him really proud.

DOI: 10.4324/9781003207986-15

All the parents were gathering under the shelter that was used for lunch and assemblies, and Wesley felt a rush of joy as he saw Simon approaching the class, smiling broadly. Isla was the first to run over and hug him, and then apologise, worried that she had hurt his arm, which was in plaster from shoulder to wrist. Everyone else flooded around him, cheering and chattering, and in some cases wiping tears from their eyes. Wesley hung back, feeling shy, but Simon's eyes found him, looking over Neil's head as he hugged him like a limpet round his waist. They nodded and smiled at each other with no need to speak. When the assembly started, Simon and Wesley sat next to each other and received enthusiastic applause when they gave their short speeches. Mrs Omwoto handed out various prizes for achievement during the year. Simon won the overall prize for sport and Isla won the academic prize. The smaller children were becoming restless when Mrs Omwoto stood up for the last time and began to speak.

"This year, we have a new prize that has not been presented at the school before. The Morgan Prize for bravery and determination has been kindly donated by Mr and Mrs Morgan, Simon Morgan's parents. It is to be awarded to the student who has worked the hardest to overcome difficulties and make a positive contribution to the school. This year's outstanding winner has shown tremendous grit and willpower, to become the young man he is today. In the last week, he has shown exceptional loyalty, courage and intelligence in saving the life of one of his classmates. It is with enormous pleasure that I award this prize to Wesley

MacKay!" The school hall erupted with applause; the children thumped their feet on the floor and adults stood up, calling and whistling as they clapped. Wesley sat in his place, feeling a little confused by everyone's reaction, until Simon prodded him out of his seat.

"Go on!" he shouted over the din. "This is your moment."

Wesley walked up the aisle to where Mrs Omwoto stood smiling, ready to shake his hand. She handed over the most beautiful wooden carving of a soaring eagle, before hugging him tightly yet again. Wesley winced. He had never been so hugged in all his life, and having broken ribs wasn't making it much fun. But he couldn't help smiling and he turned to face the crowd. They were still roaring applause. He could see his father surreptitiously wiping away a tear on the sleeve of his uniform. Anna was crying unashamedly, while clapping as furiously as her husband. All the teachers were on their feet, cheering, and he could see Simon's parents standing near the back, smiling and clapping as hard as everyone else. Mrs Morgan blew him a kiss and Wesley's ears went pink. Then Mr Morgan strode up the aisle towards the stage. For a second, Wesley considered fleeing across the back of the stage to avoid yet another terrifying encounter with Simon's father. But Mr Morgan was smiling broadly and suddenly did not look alarming anymore. In front of the whole school, he grasped Wesley's hand and shook it firmly.

"Thank you," he said. "Thank you from the bottom of my heart."

"It's a pleasure," Wesley replied.

Epilogue

Isla woke early on New Year's Day when the sun was just beginning to peep over the mountain. She slipped out of bed and went out on to the balcony, watching Mount Kenya's silhouette gradually appear out of the gloom. She couldn't see them, of course. But she knew they were there, and her heart told her that they were fine.

She was right. A couple of thousand metres above her, four figures stood together on the summit, gazing in awe at the beautiful paradise spreading away below them in all directions. As the sun yawned over the horizon, they removed their hats and scarves, and it became obvious that the group was made up of two fathers and two sons. The first pair were tall, blond and athletically slim beneath their layers of clothes. The father walked with a slight limp, but nothing could mask the joy on his face as he repeatedly hugged the boys and shook the other man's hand. The other pair were of a shorter, stocky build. Both had deep chestnut-brown hair; the man's was cropped short, but the boy's looked like a nest of sticks pointing

 DOI: 10.4324/9781003207986-16

in all directions, after having been crammed in a hat all morning. He had deep brown eyes and smooth brown skin. But the most striking thing about him was his smile. People had tended not to notice Wesley's smile when he had been obese. His weight had been his defining feature. Now, what others noticed was his mischievous smile.

Simon's father pulled a hip flask from his pocket and called the others' attention. "I would like to propose a toast," he announced. "To faithful friends!"

"To faithful friends," they all cheered.

Simon looked back down the path that they had clambered up in the pre-dawn night. It stretched away below them, twisting for miles towards the horizon.

"The problem is," he sighed, "we've now got to walk all the way back down."

"Aha!" teased Wesley. "Maybe not!" He delved into his rucksack and pulled out a small round tea tray. It was slightly frilly round the edges and had a picture of Her Majesty Queen Elizabeth II, sitting delicately in her state robes.

"I think it's time to take Isla's advice and go down Mount Kenya on a tea tray!" said Wesley. Simon bellowed with laughter as the two fathers looked completely mystified.

"Wes, have you been carrying a tray around with you for five days?" asked his dad. "You're bonkers!"

"Tea tray for two, leaving shortly," replied Wesley, talking through his nose like a train announcement.

"Wait for me. I'm coming!" replied his friend.